Routledge Revivals

Educational Change and Social Transformation

Since the fall of the Berlin Wall in 1989, the East German educational system has undergone fundamental changes within the context of a vast restructuring of the economy, the political system, and the institutions of civil society. These changes affect the very core of what goes on in teaching and learning at schools and universities. First published in 1996, *Educational Change and Social Transformation* provides an account of the nature and extent of these changes from both a policy and a classroom perspective, showing how every facet of education—governance, curriculum, structure, and teaching—has been profoundly affected by the transformation of the social and political environment.

The authors are a team of American and German researchers, some of whom have also been participant actors in the process of change that this book analyses. Their analysis should appeal to educational practitioners, policy makers, and researchers alike, as well as to those interested in better understanding the nature of the transformation that swept through Central and Eastern Europe.

Educational Change and Social Transformation

Teachers, Schools and Universities in Eastern Germany

Hans N. Weiler, Heinrich Mintrop and Elisabeth Fuhrmann

First published in 1996
by The Falmer Press

This edition first published in 2025 by Routledge
4 Park Square, Milton Park, Abingdon, Oxon, OX14 4RN

and by Routledge
605 Third Avenue, New York, NY 10158

Routledge is an imprint of the Taylor & Francis Group, an informa business

© H.N. Weiler, H.A. Mintrop, and E. Fuhrmann, 1996

All rights reserved. No part of this book may be reprinted or reproduced or utilised in any form or by any electronic, mechanical, or other means, now known or hereafter invented, including photocopying and recording, or in any information storage or retrieval system, without permission in writing from the publishers.

Publisher's Note
The publisher has gone to great lengths to ensure the quality of this reprint but points out that some imperfections in the original copies may be apparent.

Disclaimer
The publisher has made every effort to trace copyright holders and welcomes correspondence from those they have been unable to contact.

A Library of Congress record exists under LCCN: 95023278

ISBN: 978-1-041-14807-4 (hbk)
ISBN: 978-1-003-67626-3 (ebk)
ISBN: 978-1-041-14810-4 (pbk)

Book DOI 10.4324/9781003676263

Educational Change and Social Transformation:
Teachers, Schools and Universities in Eastern Germany

Hans N. Weiler
Heinrich Mintrop
Elisabeth Fuhrmann

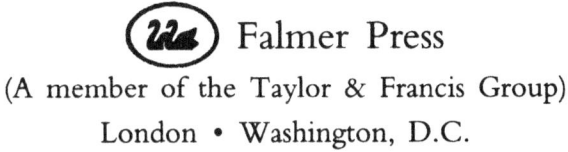 Falmer Press
(A member of the Taylor & Francis Group)
London • Washington, D.C.

UK	The Falmer Press, 4 John Street, London WC1N 2ET
USA	The Falmer Press, Taylor & Francis Inc., 1900 Frost Road, Suite 101, Bristol, PA 19007

© H.N. Weiler, H.A. Mintrop, and E. Fuhrmann, 1996

All rights reserved. No part of this publication may be reproduced, stored in a retrieval system, or transmitted in any form or by any means, electronic, mechanical, photocopying, recording or otherwise, without permission in writing from the Publisher.

First published in 1996

A catalogue record for this book is available from the British Library

Library of Congress Cataloging-in-Publication Data are available on request

ISBN 0 7507 0473 x cased
ISBN 0 7507 0474 8 paper

Jacket design by Caroline Archer

Typeset in 11/13 pt Bembo by
Graphicraft Typesetters Ltd., Hong Kong.

Printed in Great Britain by Burgess Science Press, Basingstoke on paper which has a specified pH value on final paper manufacture of not less than 7.5 and is therefore 'acid free'.

Contents

Acknowledgments		vii
Chapter 1	Introduction	1
Chapter 2	Primary and Secondary Schools in East and West Germany: An Historical Perspective	8
Chapter 3	Transforming the Content of Education: The Dynamics of Curriculum Reform in Brandenburg	22
Chapter 4	Teachers and the Democratization of Schools	37
Chapter 5	The New Structure of Secondary Schools: Macro Politics and Micro Adaptations	58
Chapter 6	Reproduction Versus Differentiation: The Politics of Higher Education	90
Chapter 7	Educational Change and Social Transformation	104
Appendix	Glossary of German Terms	115
	Diagrams of the East and West German School Systems	119
References		121
Index		129

Acknowledgments

Research of the kind reported in this book requires support from many sources, and the authors have been fortunate in being assisted by many individuals and institutions on both sides of the Atlantic. We are especially indebted to the many German teachers, administrators and students who freely shared their views and experiences with us, even where those experiences were for them sometimes a source of confusion and uncertainty; their candor and patience are greatly appreciated. Special thanks go to the Ministries of Education of the states of Brandenburg and Thüringen for their assistance in conducting the study.

Generous financial support for our work has come from the Spencer Foundation of Chicago and the Fritz Thyssen Stiftung of Köln. Our respective home institutions — Stanford University, the Europa-Universität Viadrina at Frankfurt (Oder) and the Pädagogisches Landesinstitut Brandenburg (PLIB) — have supported our work in a variety of ways. By making its excellent facilities and documentary resources available to two of the authors at various points, the Max-Planck-Institut für Bildungsforschung in Berlin has contributed in no small measure to the success of this project. Professor Wolfgang Edelstein and his staff have our special thanks for their kind and efficient assistance.

All of the above have a share in whatever value this book is found to have. Its weaknesses are the authors' alone.

Chapter 1

Introduction

It has been six years now — on 9 November 1989 — that the people of the German Democratic Republic breached the Berlin Wall and swept the authoritarian socialist regime of the previous forty years aside. During these six years the East German educational system has undergone fundamental changes within the context of a vast restructuring of the economy, the political system, and the institutions of civil society. These changes affect the very core of teaching and learning in schools and universities. All of the major elements of the educational system are involved: governance, content, pedagogy, personnel and formal organizational structure.

This book provides an account of the nature and extent of these changes, and an analysis of how they relate to the wider process of social transformation that is taking place in Eastern Germany. The book has a twofold objective: it wants to inform a wider audience of educators in the English-speaking world about an instance of social and educational change in one of the major countries of the 'new Europe', and it seeks to present new knowledge about the conditions and modalities of educational change in a period of broad social transformation. At a time when 'systemic change' has prominently appeared on the reform agenda of the United States, this book will illustrate a case of the complete and rather unprecedented remake of an entire educational system. In the process, it will look at both the policy level, where far-reaching goals are set, and at the level of practice in schools where these goals are to be enacted in the mundane world of everyday professional routine. The book will thus shed light on the nature of educational change from a systems perspective as well as from the perspective of the teacher. The varied frames of looking at change should appeal to educational practitioners, policy makers, and researchers alike, as well as to those interested in better understanding the nature of the transformation that has been sweeping through Central and Eastern Europe in recent years. Within this broader historical context, the Eastern Germany of today provides a veritable laboratory of large-scale educational and social change. It is hoped that the book will help educators in the US and other countries to take advantage of this unique opportunity for studying educational change as it is unfolding before our very eyes.

The book consists of seven chapters that are for the most part based on four studies undertaken within the framework of an ongoing research project on Eastern German education funded by the Spencer Foundation and the Fritz Thyssen Stiftung. The studies target major elements of the educational system and rely on data from observations, interviews and documents. The authors are a team of American and German researchers, some of whom have also been participating actors in the process of change that this book analyzes. While the first three studies deal with secondary schools, the fourth one investigates higher education and offers an interesting contrast to the situation in secondary schools. Findings from the studies are complemented by a compilation of pertinent background and descriptive information drawn from a variety of sources. Earlier accounts of the studies' findings have been presented by the authors at a variety of professional meetings and seminars.

Eastern Germany in Transition

Eastern Germany today is a society in transition from authoritarian socialism towards the pluralist and capitalist society that had developed in Western Germany. While the initial liberalization of the communist regime in the fall of 1989 was characterized by a preponderance of grassroots action, the dynamic of social change subsequently shifted to a preponderance of the state. The first phase, characterized by an open search for a new, as yet unknown democratic socialism, was upstaged by a second and current phase of transition to a known model, the society of the West, via the immediate adoption and incorporation of democratic and market-economic institutions into the fabric of Eastern German social life (Zapf, 1992, p. 11). But the imitation and appropriation of this model by the East German society has proven to be extremely taxing. If fertility rates may serve as an indicator of public sentiment and public stress, then the situation could not be more dramatic. On the territory of the former GDR, these rates have plunged to levels even far below the ones that were seen during the immediate post-World War II era when Germany was physically and morally in complete shambles (*ibid*, p. 3). Moreover, scholars estimate that in 1990/91 about half of the work force in Eastern Germany changed jobs or lost them, and that presently about two thirds of the work force is either unemployed or occupies insecure positions (*ibid*, p. 6). But not all sectors of society are equally affected. Schools, on the whole, retained their personnel, except for about 10 per cent of the teaching force who had lost their jobs by the 1991/92 school term (Schmidt, 1991).

In mid-1990, the accelerated unification process had consummated the brief period of 'popular upsurge' (O'Donnell and Schmitter, 1986, p. 53) and relegated 'the citizen groups and political movements that produced the East German revolution' (Dalton, 1991, p. 26) to the periphery. Although the democratic movement was able to take center stage for a short period after the repressive state apparatus began crumbling, some scholars (Offe, 1991; Pollack, 1990) point out that the East German revolution was from the beginning as much a 'voice revolution' as it was an 'exit revolution' that was triggered by external changes:

> No victorious, collective struggle for a new political order ended the GDR; only a passive emigration of individuals that could be prevented no longer destroyed its economic basis. (...) At bottom was a lack of moral and political involvement on the part of the GDR population: it did not emerge as the winner of a revolution but as a bankrupt estate under new management. (Offe, 1991, p. 26)

The ensuing unification process, repeatedly legitimated by a huge majority of the East German population, has turned out to be a rather erratic economic absorption by Western public and private entities and a more planned incorporation of the East through legal and administrative means (von Beyme, 1991).

Thus, the present transition in Eastern Germany reveals a two-sided process: the superimposition of Western legal and cultural norms and organizational forms from above, and an adaptation of Eastern individual and collective actors in their beliefs and practices to these processes of institutional change. The two sides of the process are time-incongruent, institutional time running a faster clock (Giesen und Leggewie, 1991).

It is this unusual coexistence of full-scale systemic change according to a 'proven model' and the retention of the old teaching force, culturally steeped in the vanished GDR society, that creates such an intriguing opportunity for studying the reaction of teachers — as micropolitical actors, so to speak — to major changes in their professional and political environment. Incidentally, the swiftness and completeness of the institutional change process distinguishes Eastern Germany from other countries of the former Eastern bloc that, for better or worse, cannot rely on a readily available 'proven model' and have to chart their own national course of institutional development.

The imposition-adaptation configuration is the common theme around which the various studies revolve that are the basis of this book. This configuration comes into view on both the level of policy formation and the level of policy implementation and actual educational practices. Theories on the legitimacy of the modern state, on democratization, and on educational policy implementation guide this dual-level analysis.

What the literature on the modern democratic state suggests is a conspicuous degree of vacillation between two political objectives that are competing with one another: the state's need for maintaining control over the policy process, in our case presumably for the sake of institutional isomorphism between East and West and, the recognition that participation and democratization would substantially enhance the state's credibility and legitimacy. It is this dilemma, we argue, that forms the basis of what we have called 'the politics of ambivalence'.

As our investigations show, this tension between control, and democratic legitimation is a helpful notion in understanding the contestation around the issue of 'educational federalism' in the new, unified Germany: the conflict arises between, accommodating the different conditions and traditions in the Eastern part of the country through greater decentralization and local participation and, on the other hand, forging a truly unified and integrated country through more centralized governance and homogenization. The book uncovers instances of Eastern autonomy as well as Western domination.

The way this tension plays itself out may be decisive for the democratic prospects of the Eastern part of the country, even of Germany as a whole. We know from democratization theory (Almond and Verba, 1963) that democracy as a political system thrives where it can rest on a culture in which citizens strike a balance between a sense of allegiance to the institutional order and a sense of being participant actors in the various institutions of society. Schools are germane in this regard. A look in the daily papers, with their reports of widespread right-wing activism, dramatically illustrates the gravity of this issue and demonstrates how far the 'new Germany' has yet to go in developing truly democratic conditions throughout the country.

The imposition-adaptation configuration also refers to another body of literature that has investigated the problematic connection between macro and micro levels in the implementation of educational reform. Its point of departure is the observation that a profusion of reform policies contrasts with a dearth of actual changes in educational practice in schools and classrooms (Cuban, 1990 and 1992). Several theories explain why this may be so.

1 Societal explanations see the efficacy of state action hampered by fundamental structural contradictions of society which the state has to manage. For instance, constant conflicts emerge around issues of 'equity' versus 'excellence', or of social integration versus selection based on ability or status. Thus ambiguous or contradictory educational policies ensue, making effective implementation uncertain (Carnoy and Levin, 1985; Weiler, 1989).
2 Organizational explanations see educational systems as loosely coupled

(Weick, 1976 and 1982) which makes central control of the system, for instance by reform-minded authorities, difficult. Loose coupling allows educational organizations, such as schools or universities, to shore up public confidence and legitimacy in the face of ever shifting and conflicting demands of the public while at the same time maintaining a degree of technical stability. Meyer and Rowan (1977 and 1978) observed that the educational system is loosely coupled in substance (for example, instructional matters), but tightly coupled in formal structure (for example, classifications and sorting mechanisms) that spell out the rationalized myths on which the legitimacy of a society's economic stratification depends.

3   Cultural explanations stress the depth of behavior regularities and routines that are presumed to be ingrained in school practice. These behavior regularities are imbued with power relationships among actors participating in schools and are difficult to reach and to change by legal and administrative means. This makes for the 'intractability' of schools to change (Sarason, 1990). Educational change is 'technically simple and socially complex' (Fullan, 1982, p. 54). Meaningful educational change is a cultural learning process for both adults and students that creates dissonance and anxiety for individuals in the 'capricious world' of schools. Much change will happen unplanned as cultural values and norms of a society change.

Two conclusions for educational policy are drawn from the tenuous link between macro and micro levels of the educational system. Some scholars question the wisdom and effect of a top-down approach to educational change (McLaughlin, 1990). In this view, local variation and adaptation of central policies are the rule in the field of education; active 'ownership' of the reform by teachers and other local actors is essential for 'real' or 'meaningful' change (Fullan, 1991). A similar change model underlies the German discussion on the school site as the unit of educational change (Steffens and Bargel, 1993; Fend, 1977).

Other authors (Huberman and Miles, 1984; Marsh and Odden, 1991) attempt to remedy the tenuous link between political and administrative leadership of state agencies and educational practice by constructing a more fine-grained model that combines crucial teacher decision-making domains with policy instruments (Schwille et al, 1988; see also Elmore and Sykes, 1992).

What makes the Eastern German case so interesting for this debate is the fact that it deviates from the American and Western European cases that underlie these theories in two crucial ways: (a) the scope of institutional or systemic change within the educational system is much more encompassing;

and (b) educational change proceeds in the context of fundamental society-wide change as overnight Westernization of the institutional order seeks to reverse forty years of socialism of that part of Germany. Will we find Eastern German educators on the move, prodded by 'systemic' levers and steeped in the ferment of a new society, or will they be stuck, wedded to the past in the face of an overwhelming, imposed, and often contradictory new institutional reality?

The following chapters of the book will approach this question by focussing on certain aspects of the broader picture. Bewildered witnesses to history in the making, we will leave the rendering of the whole picture to future projects that will have gained greater distance from the momentous events of the past six years.

The Organization of the Book

It will be useful for the reader to become acquainted first with some broad similarities and differences between the Western and Eastern German educational systems. Thus the chapter following these introductory remarks presents the historical development of primary and secondary schools in comparative perspective. This will help clarify the point of departure for change after the demise of the GDR regime and the direction this process will take. The issues that loom large in this overview include individualism versus collectivism, pluralism versus unitarianism, mobility and stratification, teacher professionalism, and mutual enemy images. While a review from an historical distance facilitates the presentation of the educational system as a unity of philosophy, organizational structures, teaching technologies, and personnel, the subsequent chapters reporting on present developments emphasize separate aspects of the system.

Chapter 3 on curriculum reform describes changes in the curricular frameworks of a number of subjects during the last year of the GDR and the first few years in the policy life of one newly-constituted Land (state). Intentions, actors, and procedures on the governmental level are analyzed as part of the conflict between rapid assimilation to the West and maintenance of Eastern autonomy, and between state control over, and legitimation of, the intended curriculum.

In chapter 4 on teachers and the democratization of schools, the analysis turns to actual secondary school sites. The claims of the new educational authorities for greater democratization are investigated from the perspective of teachers who for the most part retained their tenure and who are now to fill the new democratic institutions with life. It is found that in the thicket of everyday interaction at school sites democratization is an immensely

Introduction

ambivalent process that involves educators in a painful redistribution of authority among teachers, students and parents, and the state's authorities.

Chapter 5 on the new structure of secondary schools analyzes the scope of reorganization that took place as a result of the structural adjustments of Eastern comprehensive schools to the Western three-track system of secondary schooling. Teachers in newly formed lower-track and upper-track schools are visited and their ways of coping with the new school types and of adapting them to their previous experience are examined. A surprising willingness to operate tracks and a strong durability of traditional assumptions are found.

While both the reform of curriculum and school practices can be seen as a delicate balancing act between institutional imposition and local adaptation, higher education starkly deviates from this configuration. Chapter 6 on the politics of higher education shows that this sector experienced a 'cloning' along the lines of Western institutions of higher education to a much larger degree. Not only are formal organizational structures and curricula adopted, but a substantial exchange of personnel also takes place as a large number of Eastern scholars are replaced by newly-recruited Western academics.

A reflection on educational change and social transformation in comparative perspective in chapter 7 concludes our analysis.

It should be added here that, for the most part, the manuscript of this book was written in late 1993 and early 1994, with some final editing in the early summer of 1994. Clearly, in a process such as the one we are studying, conditions change with remarkable speed and sometimes in unforeseen directions. Nonetheless, by the time this book went to press, we had satisfied ourselves that the policy decisions and educators' reactions on which our analysis focuses were firmly enough in place validly to serve as the empirical basis of our conclusions. As the transformation of the educational system in Eastern Germany continues, the significance of this crucial period immediately following unification for the further development of the system should become even more obvious.

Chapter 2

Primary and Secondary Schools in East and West Germany: An Historical Perspective

Wolfgang Mitter (1981) once remarked that 'the recent German history of education is an example of how within a relatively short period of time traditional bonds dissolve and even disappear, how, in short, one German educational system becomes two' (p. 11). It is now time to add the question of how those two become one again. It is difficult to gauge how far West and East had drifted apart and thus what distance they will need to travel in order to reconstitute the educational system of one unified nation.

Similarities and differences are relatively easy to establish for the level of organizational structure, governance, laws and official curricula. Various comparative studies (Hearnden, 1974; Baske, 1981; Fishman and Martin, 1987; Anweiler, 1990) are available on those aspects of schooling. The picture becomes murkier, however, for the actual stuff of schools: teaching and learning in classrooms, the interaction between adults and youths, or the general school climate. Here, the official point of view is a poor guide. Brown and Gray (1984), in analyzing communist political culture, makes a distinction between 'official' and 'dominant' culture, the latter being de facto in peoples' minds. A similar 'double culture' presumably did and still does pervade schools, more so in the former GDR than in the old Federal Republic of (West) Germany.

But ethnographic studies that would be useful for comparing Western with Eastern 'dominant' school cultures are not available. Particularly in the case of the GDR, what went on between teachers and students in reality has to be illuminated by hindsight, through inferences, anecdotal evidence, and *a posteriori* reconstruction, opening up a new and difficult field of research. The following comparative sketch acknowledges this difficulty and limits itself largely to an investigation of goals, structures, teaching content, and instructional methods in schools. Our picture owes much to the insightful study by Fishman and Martin (1987), even though our emphasis will bias this picture towards difference. For, both systems operated under a reverse enemy image that eagerly stressed being a positive contrast to the other.

Anti-communism in the West and anti-capitalism in the East were important ideological planks of the respective educational systems.

'.... How One German Educational System Becomes Two'

Although both systems hail from the same educational roots, adhered to many elements of a German national heritage, and share a common language, they espoused very different educational and political philosophies for roughly forty years that resulted in divergent structures and curricula. Yet, the process of growing apart always contained elements of convergence that came to the fore in various reform phases, most notably the lessening of elitism and the introduction of polytechnic elements in the Western system during the sixties and seventies, and the reintroduction of the 'bourgeois-progressive heritage' and the promotion of special schools for highly gifted students in the Eastern system during the seventies and eighties. In addition, despite a great deal of reform certain features remained at the core of both systems: a relatively strong emphasis on general education in secondary schools, the venerable institution of the 'Abitur' as the entrance ticket to university studies, and the dual structure of apprenticeship education in vocational school and work place.

West Germany[1]

It is the primary task of schools in the Western view to develop individuals to their fullest potential who then contribute to the betterment of the society. In this endeavor, schools share educational authority and responsibility with the family. Schools are to present a pluralist world view, and students are to enjoy basic civil rights, such as freedom of speech and expression. They are to advance within the school system solely based on the merits of their academic performance. That, as a by-product, these principles served to reproduce the traditional class structure of the country was obvious but less acknowledged. It was not until the 'Bildungsreform' of the late sixties and seventies that education was seen as a vehicle of social reconstruction and a serious effort was launched to correct social inequalities through education.

In West Germany, no clear educational consensus exists beyond the basic tenets of individualism, pluralism and meritocracy. Generally speaking, the country is divided into two main camps of educational policy, one pursuing a more progressive, the other a more conservative, agenda. The progressive agenda, as we call it here, is an agenda of reform. It stresses preparation for life in a constantly changing world; social involvement, political responsibility; . . . an appreciation and understanding of modern science; . . . structural changes so that advanced secondary and higher education would no longer be the domain of a small group of elite citizens. (Fishman and Martin, 1987, p. 67)

Thus progressives advocate modernism, individual specialization, and social integration in schools. Often, comprehensive schools (*Gesamtschulen*) that are to educate students from all social classes and of all abilities in the same school are the progressives' preferred school type. Progressives are mainly organized in the political parties of the left, in the teacher union affiliated with the labor movement, and in citizen organizations close to that spectrum.

Conservatives, for their part, contend that the traditional German three-tier system, dating back a century or so (Friedeburg, 1992), with a college-preparatory Gymnasium, a technical-clerical oriented Realschule, and a manual labor oriented Hauptschule (formerly Volksschule), has served the country well in its successful adaptation to new technological challenges. For them, the economic success of the country speaks for itself. Conservatives are anxious to preserve academic standards and a core of general education ('Allgemeinbildung') for each achievement level. This is to be insured by early selection and channeling of students, preferably after the fourth grade.

Conservatives advocate a strong vocational track that stresses the formative influence of apprenticeship training at the work place, but foremost they are the stalwarts of the Gymnasium as an institution of traditional humanism and elite education that rightfully confers a special social status on the ones that manage to leave it with the Abitur in hand (i.e., the admission ticket to a university). Conservatives mainly gravitate toward right-of-center parties and the professional organizations of Gymnasium teachers. They can count on support from business leaders and the churches (particularly the Catholic church) as well as a strong sentiment of support among middle class parents (Friedeburg, 1992).

The current educational system in Western Germany is a compromise between these two camps, though one that seems to be slanted in favor of the conservative agenda. The traditional three-tier structure is a reality for the overwhelming majority of parents and students in Western Germany. The school reforms of the 60s and 70s failed to establish comprehensive schools as an alternative of equal standing (Weiler, 1989). Where these schools exist they very often fit into the prevalent three-tier structure as a kind of first/second tier super-institution.

The Gymnasium remains the unchallenged cornerstone for a regular academic career. But it has lost its monopoly, a good part of its elitism, and its monolithic curriculum (Philipp and Witjes, 1982). Although it still favors the upper strata of society, the lower strata have made in-roads. By making entrance requirements more flexible, strengthening parental influence, and diversifying curricula tailored to specific interests and aptitudes, the Gymnasium has become the school for about a third of the student population in Western Germany, up from 7 per cent in 1968 (Der Spiegel, 46, 23, p. 41). Concomitantly, universities have evolved from elite to mass institutions of higher learning. While the Gymnasium still lays the general academic foundations for university specializations — there is, after all, no general studies requirement in West German universities —, the core curriculum has been relaxed in favor of special concentrations and electives in grades 11 through 13. Parallel to the expansion of the Gymnasium, the Hauptschule, envisioned as the 'main school' (in literal translation) for post-elementary students, has been reduced to a residual school ('Restschule') for the 'remainder', while a Realschule education has become the standard (Statistisches Bundesamt, 1992, p. 425).

The political pluralism of the country is reflected in the variation that occurs from school to school and region to region. The Federal Republic of Germany — old as well as new — leaves educational policy making in the domain of the states or Länder. As a result, traditionally Christian-democratic (CDU) governed states (for example, the two southern states of Bavaria and Baden-Württemberg) took a more conservative stance while traditionally Social-democratic (SPD) governed states (for example, North Rhine-Westphalia and Hesse) implemented more progressive policy agendas. The effect of these policy variations is reflected in the rate of students attending a Gymnasium (only 18 per cent in Bavaria, roughly one third in North Rhine-Westphalia [Der Spiegel, 46, 23, p. 56]).

Although federal in structure, decentralization in educational governance does not extend as far as in the United States with its tradition of community control through locally elected school boards. In West Germany, citizens can influence education at the state level, which requires a fairly high degree of interest organization, and at the level of the individual school. Here, parents have a legal right of co-determination in some areas of school management exercised through the joint faculty-parent school conference.

Concurring with the German tradition of a 'strong state', many aspects of West German school life are regulated by state law or ministerial directive (for example, expenditures, curricular frameworks, promotion requirements, report cards, test and lesson schedules, shared decision-making, all the way to the proper way of addressing students: until ninth grade the informal 'Du' and first name, beginning with tenth grade the formal 'Sie' and last name). Some of these items would likely be left to the community or the school site in less regulated and centralized countries like the United States.

The state governments pay particularly close attention to the formal elements of schooling. By contrast, the actual delivery of the curriculum is left up to the discretion and professional authority of teachers and schools. As in the United States, the supervision and accountability of teachers is poorly developed. Teachers in Western Germany select textbooks (from a state approved list) and teaching materials and design teaching units that correspond to the loosely worded state curriculum framework. They are expected to decide what instructional methods are most suitable for their classes. They may also present their own points of view, but are mandated to do this in the context of a balanced picture. Parents' prerogatives have to be taken into consideration as well. Truth is considered tenuous and, particularly in the humanities and social sciences, can only be recognized in inter-subjective communication which entails discussion and critical thinking as instructional features of classrooms.

The relative academic freedom in the classroom may be due as much to the liberal constitution of West German society as it may rest on the traditional professional standing of Gymnasium teachers in particular who have traditionally been part of the scholarly elite of German society (Friedeburg, 1992). This status is ardently guarded by the Gymnasium teachers, but other categories of teachers, previously trained at special three-year schools of education, have successfully inched closer to that elevated status, for example by also graduating from university programs.

The reform movement of the seventies introduced many educational innovations to the teaching profession that emphasize a student-centered pedagogy, such as cooperative learning, project instruction, discovery learning, and a less authoritarian concept of the teacher's role. This type of pedagogy has become the norm for teacher education programs. The incidence of these instructional methods in the daily practice of West German schools will vary considerably according to school type and state.

East Germany[2]

The political and educational orientation of the German Democratic Republic (GDR) was basically collectivist. Individuals were to develop in harmony with the overall goal of creating a new classless society. In the new classless society fascism was to be eradicated once and for all. While, from the Eastern point of view, former Nazi elites had been in control again in the West shortly after the war, turning a blind eye to Nazism for the sake of a vigorous anti-communism, the GDR was supposedly ruled by democrats and anti-fascists who had experienced resistance and concentration camps. The new leadership felt compelled to destroy the capitalist breeding ground of fascism in their part of the country. Anti-fascism became a guiding idea for schools early on in the GDR. But the Nazi period was treated as a primarily social-structural phenomenon, not as an everyday occurrence of allegiance, oppression, and racism of ordinary people. Thus the revolutionary break with the past and the creation of a new socialist order was seen as absolving East Germans of the uncomfortable ownership of this dark historical chapter (Lepenies, 1992).

The new classless society required a transition period during which the working class was to become the dominating class. The educational system was therefore to provide opportunities for working class youth to rise to the top of the economic and social ladder. The separation of planning from execution in production that exploited and alienated workers under the capitalist division of labor had to be abolished. Instead, it was the task of the educational system to work towards the integration of intellectual and manual labor and to create the 'all-round developed socialist personality' as a new type of human being.

The new socialist order was to unleash productive forces by way of rational planning and by liberating the dormant potential of the actual producers of goods. For the 'scientific-technological revolution' to happen, the East German educational system was to provide an ample supply of qualified manpower and professional cadres for the 'people-owned' socialist economy.

The collective goals of the socialist society were embodied in the state and the communist party. The Marxist-Leninist party was the 'avantgarde' that prodded the masses along towards its vision of a better future. It was an elite minority with tenuous support in society that demanded allegiance to its rule. Thus, the educational system had a triple role to play: (i) it had to guarantee the economic development of society; (ii) it had to induce the restructuring of the class structure; and (iii) it had to insure not just allegiance to the will of the party, but preferably active participation and vigilance in the execution of its goals. Structure, content, and instructional methods of schooling in the GDR flowed from these goals.

It took the party about twenty years to overcome the remnants of the traditional German three-tier system and to create the unitary polytechnical school ('Polytechnische Oberschule (POS)') that almost every East German student attended from grade 1 to grade 10. In this unitary school students were taught in heterogeneous core groups; tracking was not permitted, electives were few (Fischer, 1992, p. 64). After the tenth grade, most students were channelled into various forms of vocational training organized within units of socialist production. About 10 per cent of the students, selected on the basis of grades and political attitudes ('fester Klassenstandpunkt'), spent two additional years in the extended secondary school ('Erweiterte Oberschule

(EOS)') and achieved the Abitur, i.e., university admission (Waterkamp, 1987; Fischer, 1992, p. 65).

The unitary character of the polytechnical school, instruction in socialist production, a vocational stream to acquire the Abitur and reach the university, and preferential treatment of working class youth in the nomination for the Extended Secondary School (Waterkamp, 1987) all contributed to the initial success with which the socialist state opened up higher education to the social classes previously excluded from it. In the mid-fifties, the GDR announced that about 53 per cent of all university students came from working class backgrounds. The comparable Western figure at the time was 4 per cent (Hearnden, 1974, p. 86). In addition, women entered the work force and reached qualified positions in ever higher numbers.

The tremendous mobility in the East was partly due to the fact that more and more members of the upper and middle classes lost their traditional means of living and often migrated to the West causing shortages of highly qualified labor. This initial upward mobility in the young GDR could not be maintained in subsequent decades. For one, the erection of the Berlin Wall in 1961 made a further exodus from the East virtually impossible. But more importantly, and contrary to ideological pretence, the GDR school system began to reproduce a new socialist bureaucracy and intelligentsia once those strata had established themselves in the post-war years. Thus, already in the seventies access to vocational streams leading to higher learning was restricted due to an anticipated lower demand for higher qualifications (Lemke, 1991). After all, the GDR government guaranteed employment commensurate to one's educational status. Thus, the unitary system did not create equality. Geißler (1990, p. 8) estimates that only between 12 and 15 per cent of the 1982 university entering class were children of industrial workers, though many more students were classified as 'working class'. This was due to the fact that all party and state employees were entitled to this desirable working class label. In the eighties, then, the odds of gaining access to higher education in the GDR for almost all social strata can be estimated to have become smaller than in the West with its reformed school system. Indeed, as Lemke (1991, p. 115) points out, a conspicuous number of migrants from the GDR to the West in the summer and autumn of 1989 gave as a reason for leaving the GDR that their children faced restricted educational and professional futures. Thus, for the contemporary teacher and parent generation in the East early tracking of a large number of students is a novelty, while the selection of a small political-academic elite presumably is not (Klier, 1990; Waterkamp, 1990 and 1987; Fischer, 1992).

Educational policy-making and governance emanated directly from the upper echelons of the Socialist Unity Party (SED). Usually the party spoke with one voice. Existing opposition to the official party line, for example in the debate on the restructuring of the three-tier system, was muted and denounced as revisionist or bourgeois (Hearnden, 1974, p. 132). The party line was executed through the Leninist principle of 'democratic centralism' which allowed for input from the lower levels of the state and party apparatus and from mass organizations, but demanded of them obedience once a directive was issued from a higher level of the hierarchy. With the abolition of the federal structure in the East in 1952, schools were directly governed from (East) Berlin. They were supervised by both state officials and party secretaries. Clandestine surveillance through the state secret service ('Stasi') was common (*Frankfurter Rundschau* [FR], 18 April 1991).

The philosophical foundation of schooling in the GDR was Marxism-Leninism which permeated the curriculum at all levels of education and was a required course at universities. Marxism-Leninism provided students with a comprehensive concept of the world, a guideline for social development and morality, and a justification for the leading role of the communist party. Accordingly, school knowledge consisted of certain truths, resting on a 'scientific world view', and on encompassing knowledge structures, coverage of which followed a sequential and encyclopedic order.

A cornerstone of the unitary school was its polytechnical element. Through useful work in productive units in conjunction with instruction, all students — prospective workers and intellectuals alike — were to integrate theory and practice, become acquainted with the world of work, and learn from the working class as the leading class in society. Another obligatory subject that was added to the curriculum in the late seventies was military instruction (Fischer, 1992, p. 110). It was to reinforce a perception of the West as the class enemy, increase students' identification with the GDR and their willingness to defend socialism side by side with the 'Soviet brothers'. Bitter protest by the Protestant church and other groups against this militarization of education was to no avail.

In GDR schools, a view of education prevailed that saw learning and instruction as scientific, non-experiential, and teacher-centered. The teacher dispensed a unified, preplanned curriculum in 45-minute segments to stable classes with very little external or internal differentiation.

> In the instructional process of the German democratic school, as an organized process of learning and educating, theory is assigned the leading role, and the students' personal component is assigned the secondary role. (Directive on the Lesson as the Foundation of School Work..., 1950, cited in Uhlig, 1970, p. 365)

This theory as well as its interpretations as rendered by the party leadership were translated into educational objectives from which the 'correct' pedagogical content and method derived. Teachers were to lead the learning of their students in the direction of the prescribed societal goals. The student's personality was seen as a product of circumstance and planned education (Rudolf, 1990, p. 915). Content matter and curricular goals took precedence over considerations of suitable child-centered methods.

But this does not mean that students were to function as merely passive recipients of the curriculum. Instead, revolutionary fervor and commitment to socialism was encouraged as well as active participation — often measured by students' involvement in the state youth organization which had a strong official presence in all schools. Teachers were to rouse students, but had to see to it that the party line would triumph in the end. Parents' sentiments paled in the face of these mandates. Learning took place in stable core groups and learning collectives, and individual problems or misbehavior were often worked out involving these groups.

Teachers, though supposedly leaders in their classrooms, were tightly supervised by administrators, and followed a curriculum ('Lehrplan') planned for them in detail through textbooks, lesson plans, and other teaching aids, and monitored by mentor teachers ('Fachberater'). The 'Lehrplan' for the polytechnical secondary school is more than 4000 pages long (Drewelow, 1990, p. 200). Teachers' faithfulness to the Lehrplan was reportedly very high (*ibid*). In general, opposition or criticism on the part of teachers beyond a very limited degree was not tolerated by the authorities, and if it occurred it would lead in many instances to a loss of the job (Klier, 1990).

Teachers were trained for their role in schools of education that operated with the same kind of tight curriculum and organization that was common in their future work places. Prospective as well as practicing teachers alike were expected to be heavily involved in political and community activities conducted by the party or the official mass organizations. In addition, participation in special ideological in-service training organized by the party was mandatory. Although East German teachers functioned in a tightly constrained environment devoid of academic freedom, their professional judgment within the confines of this space was weighty. For example, a teacher's comprehensive evaluation of a student's personality could advance a student's academic career or could relegate a student to special education classes without parents' recourse to objective criteria (for example, tests) or legal means. Conduct (for example, political and moral reliability), rather than achievement alone determined students' advancement (*ibid*).

East German schools were 'tight' organizations, but since taught ideology and social reality contradicted each other in too many ways, goal achievement tended to be ritualistic. Many teachers and particularly students learned to live with a 'double truth, one for the school, and one for life' (Kiefer, 1990, p. 790). Despite great ideological efforts, schools succeeded less and less in creating the desired identification of students with the socialist order. According to only recently published survey data, East German youths' positive attitudes peaked in the mid-1970s (roughly half believed in Socialism then), but declined precipitously thereafter, particularly after 1985 when *perestroika* began in the Soviet Union, and evaporated altogether in the late eighties (Lemke, 1991, pp. 104–11).

Apart from a gap between what was and what ought to be, East German pedagogy was plagued by another contradiction. The school system had originally set out to eliminate traditional social inequalities and to impart the comprehensive ideology of the party. East Germans were to be socialized into stable, non-competitive collective forms of interaction that were guided by internalized values of solidarity and compliance. On the other hand, competition with the economically stronger West as well as its own claim of being the superior system forced the GDR to mobilize for the 'scientific-technological revolution'. This entailed the early selection and special treatment of highly gifted students as well as an application of scientific methods (for example, creativity, exploration, individualism) in learning. Rather than opening up the system and its pedagogical rigidities, as had happened in the West, the party resolved this contradiction between necessary modernization and high performance, on the one hand, and desired compliance with the socialist order, on the other hand, by stressing technological content coupled with a massive campaign of re-ideologization (*ibid*, p. 118) and a reinforcement of party control.

'. . . How Two Educational Systems Become One Again'

Unification of the two German systems of education has turned out to be essentially a one-sided process. It consists of an assimilation of the East to Western ways. Thus the current process of change is primarily a task for the East. Two distinct phases of educational change can be distinguished in Eastern Germany that correspond with developments in the larger society. In each phase, different social actors occupy center-stage, and different change dynamics are at work. The first — which one may call the 'round table phase' of educational change — was an outgrowth of the genuine 'revolution' in the GDR, while changes in the second phase respond much more to the exigencies of accelerated unification.

The popular mass movement of the fall of 1989 that toppled the authoritarian regime of the Socialist Unity Party (SED) triggered a spontaneous movement at many schools. Students resisted dogmatic and authoritarian teachers (Oberschule 'Alfred Kurella', 1990, pp. 40–2), and teachers resisted party cadres, 'Stasi' (secret service) informants, and union stewards that were seen as tainted by their deeds under the old regime (Schreiner, 1990, p. 13). Principals were terminated and could only be brought back — which did not happen infrequently — on a vote of confidence of the whole school community, including newly-formed parent organizations (König, 1990, p. 10). All over the GDR, the communist party was stripped of its leading role, and the state youth organization was banned from the schools. Formerly obligatory instruction in Marxism-Leninism was terminated, and curricula were purged of official state doctrines.

At the local and national levels, so-called 'round tables' emerged from the grassroots movement and existed side by side with the GDR government. Key participants in these round tables came from the formerly illegal democratic grassroots organizations and churches, or were independent critical intellectuals or artists (Okun, 1990, p. 273). Though official organizations, like parties, unions etc. (Schmidt, 1990, p. 10) as well as some 'reformed' educational scholars were represented (*Frankfurter Rundschau*, 20 February 1990), teachers remained more or less on the sidelines.

The tightly regimented education sector ('Volksbildung') unfroze with some delay. This is not surprising in light of the fact that in the past teachers were particularly well oiled cogs in the authoritarian state machine of the GDR (*Frankfurter Rundschau*, 13 February 1990; Klier, 1990). Party membership was reportedly high among teachers, and allegedly one out of ten teachers was an informant of the 'Stasi' (*Frankfurter Rundschau*, 18 April 1991). The degree to which schools were at the party's beck and call may be indicated by the fact that at the height of the upheaval when the party was pressured to dismantle its security apparatus, political personnel was hastily transferred into schools — 700 'Modrow-Lehrer' (Schmidt, 1991) in Brandenburg alone. If teachers' responses in the fall of 1989 to Christa Wolf's article in *Die Wochenpost* are any indication of their sentiment towards their socialist past, then clearly defensiveness and concealed self-righteousness prevailed (Gruner, 1990).

Observers from the East (König, 1990) and the West (Schmidt, 1990) point to the initial consensus among educational reformers who envisioned a school characterized by:

(a) variation and differentiation in place of the socialist unitary school;
(b) child-centered learning, individuality, and pluralism in place of unitary ideology and state directed pedagogy;
(c) participation and decentralization in place of central bureaucratic control.

During the round table phase of educational reform accomplishments of the East German system were stressed, such as polytechnical instruction (see the testimony of the two post-SED ministers of education [Meyer, 1990, p. 1 and Abend, 1990]). On the other hand, scholars, teachers, and many parents voiced dissatisfaction with the 'straitjacket' of levelling all students, regardless of individual differences in aptitude, in the unitary polytechnical school (Kienitz, 1990, p. 107). The objections of educators to the unitary model revolved around four themes:

(i) Social conditions cannot compensate for genetic differences in human intelligence (Kaack, 1990, pp. 13–14).
(ii) The newly adopted competitive market economy needs competitive schools (Müller, 1990, p. 3).
(iii) Teachers are disillusioned and overburdened with the practice of consistently reaching out to all levels of talent and motivation (Kienitz, 1990; Heinrich, 1990, p. 765).
(iv) The unitary system did not create social equality.

However, the three-tier school system of the Federal Republic was not seen as an attractive alternative. In general, judging from a survey conducted by the Deutsche Lehrer-Zeitung (DLZ) among leading GDR educational policy-makers at the time, issues related to the organizational structure of the school system seem to have been of secondary concern at least up until the April 1990 elections in the newly created states (Große DLZ-Umfrage, 1990, pp. 3–5).

After the collapse of the communist regime, East German teachers were challenged with the redefinition of their fundamental assumptions about learning. East German education journals rediscovered the student as the subject of the learning process. The new perspective challenged teachers to design a more open classroom environment and make more autonomous decisions so as to tailor their actions to individual variations in their classrooms.

The popularity of holistic pedagogic concepts (for example, Waldorf schools, or some projects of *Reformpädagogik*) in the East German educational reform debate of 1990 (Deutsche Lehrer-Zeitung 37, 1990, p. 4) suggests a desire among educators (and parents) to fill the void that Marxism left with a different, albeit similarly all-encompassing educational philosophy. In the view of many, an alternative philosophical grounding could be provided by the wholesale adoption of West German educational models.

The reaction of the public towards the teaching force during the roundtable phase was mixed. On the one hand, the punishment of oppressive wrong-doers was demanded, but on the other hand it was recognized that a successful reform of command pedagogy and bureaucratic rigidity would have to enlist the active involvement of the classroom teachers. An honest reevaluation of the past was seen as the first step toward democratic renewal. Without coming to terms with their past, teachers could not implement the proclaimed pedagogical freedom and autonomy, nor could they expect to regain credibility and authority in the eyes of students and parents.

To sum up, the overall emphasis in the educational reform movement during the period of grassroots upheaval was on differentiating and democratizing the existing schools and overcoming forty years of 'administrative command pedagogy' (Meumann, 1990, p. 21), a term borrowed from the Soviet *perestroika* debate.

In mid-1990, the focus of educational reform shifted dramatically away from processes of awakening, self-reflection, and spontaneous action with its focus on the content of instruction and school governance. As a result of the accelerated unification process that consummated the brief period of 'popular upsurge' (O'Donnell and Schmitter, 1986, p. 53), the newly-constituted state governments in Eastern Germany became the chief actors in educational change. In the new states, the political machines of the established West German parties and state and federal educational bureaucracies gradually took center stage, bringing with them in many cases the 'unfinished business' of educational reform in the West, including the controversy between comprehensive schools and the hierarchical three-tier system. As a consequence, the battle between right-of-center and left-of-center political forces over the organizational structure of a future East German school system gained the upper hand over the reform of 'command pedagogy' in the public debate and educational policy-making arena.

In time, state governments who are constitutionally responsible for education passed major school acts (Mitter, 1992). They essentially realigned the organizational structure of the Eastern school system with that of the West German states. The formerly untracked socialist unitary school was dissolved into a separate elementary school and, on the secondary level, into a college-prep Gymnasium and middle/lower-track school types. State governments stipulated a system of co-determination in school governance while retaining supreme authority over schools in the hands of the state ministries and supreme authority over children in the hands of parents. New textbooks and curricular frameworks were adopted that introduce teachers to Western educational philosophy and content. Initially, the new Eastern school acts were copied from those Western states that provided primary 'assistance' to the Eastern ministries and were drafted by civil servants from these Western states (*Frankfurter Rundschau*, 10 January 1991). The contours of the new school system depend to a considerable degree on the policy preferences of the parties in power in the five new federal states and, as mentioned above, reflect the school war camps of the 1970s in the West. The states dominated by 'conservatives' (CDU) favored the traditional three-tier

Primary and Secondary Schools in East and West Germany

system and a resurrection of the Gymnasium while the Social Democrats (SPD) and Greens ('Die Grünen') in Brandenburg initially favored a comprehensive school system maintaining the unified organization of the polytechnical school, but allowing for differentiations within (Pädagogisches Zentrum, 1990, pp. 3–11). Eventually, the acts compromised to a certain degree with the material realities of the old system (for example, building sizes and locations), local and parental will. The result is a two-tier or three-tier structure in all new federal states. Besides lobbying activities of Western professional organizations, there is little evidence that Eastern teachers played an important role in this process. The following chapters will deal with these questions in more detail.

Notes

1 For an overview of the structure of the West German school system, see figure 2 in the appendix.
2 For an overview of the structure of the East German school system, see figure 1 in the appendix.

Chapter 3

Transforming the Content of Education: The Dynamics of Curriculum Reform in Brandenburg

Replacing curricula that served the needs of the socialist order with new ones that are designed in the spirit of the Western educational traditions of pluralism and student-centeredness is a key element in the radical reform of the Eastern German educational system. This chapter presents the results of studying in depth both process and outcome of curriculum development between late 1989 and the 1992/93 school year. This relatively short period saw a succession of precipitous events that all left their mark on school curricula: political upheaval, the demise of the communist regime, the post-communist caretaker government, and the constitution of new federal states from the beginning of regular administrative operations to the completion of a first set of curricular guidelines (*Rahmenpläne*) for the different levels of schooling. Our analysis will show how the 'intended curriculum' (Cuban, 1992) is formed and reformed by political and administrative forces in one of the new federal states in Eastern Germany, Brandenburg. How to translate the ambitious curricular change into 'taught curriculum' at school sites is a daunting challenge given the scope of the changes, the traditions of forty years of 'command pedagogy', and the limited resources of the states. It may take a few years fully to gauge the effect of these intended changes.

As was to be expected under the circumstances, this particular instance of curriculum development was subject to conflicting assumptions and influences. These conflicts have to do with both the content of the curriculum that was being developed and with the process through which it emerged. As far as the nature of the process is concerned, our study draws on one of the authors' earlier theoretical and comparative work on the legitimation of curriculum development, which emphasizes the role of participatory arrangements and the utilization of expertise in the quest for the legitimacy of the product (see Weiler, 1990). The chapter focuses on the relative role of these two strategies of legitimation, and brings out the conflict between the interests of participating teachers, the views of the subject matter experts brought in to help with the drafting of the guidelines, and the interest on the part of the Ministries of Education to maintain adequate control of the process in a period of rather considerable social and political commotion.

As far as the outcome of the process, i.e., the actual *content* of the new curriculum guidelines, is concerned, we examine the thesis that here the principal contention was between, on the one hand, following closely the curricular models of the West German *Länder* in the interest of rapid assimilation into the newly-unified country and economy and, on the other hand, pursuing a more differentiated and autonomous frame of reference that would more fully reflect Eastern traditions and specificities. In examining the curricular guidelines of the state of Brandenburg, the chapter identifies a number of critical instances where both successful and unsuccessful attempts to reconcile these competing claims become apparent. A case in point, with which the chapter deals in some detail, is the development and introduction of a new 'ethics' curriculum in Brandenburg which departs quite radically from the existing pattern of religious and moral instruction in German schools and has been at the center of a major political controversy.

In an attempt to structure the analysis of the extraordinarily complex set of materials and information that was available to us, it seemed useful to mesh the conceptual and chronological dimensions of the process of curriculum development. Conceptually, and in light of what has been said above, the three key aspects of the process are actual reform measures, the *actors* involved in the process, and the nature of the *process itself*.

The dynamic of this process suggests a distinction between two time periods:

(i) a period of initial *ad hoc* adjustments to the existing GDR curricula between the fall of the Berlin Wall on 9 November 1989 and the consummation of German unification on 3 October 1990, i.e., under the auspices of the last two GDR governments (Modrow and de Maizière); and

(ii) the period from 1991 to 1993 when these curricula were replaced (initially for ten selected subjects in primary and secondary schools) by proper new curricula for all subjects and levels of education in the state of Brandenburg (1992/93).

In each of these periods, the process of curriculum development had its own characteristic quality which reflected the political and administrative context within which education was managed during that particular period. We will seek to capture this linkage by addressing our questions about reform measures, actors and process in turn for each of the two periods.

The following is a set of theses which anticipate some of the findings of the more detailed study, but also characterize some of the questions that have guided the analysis.

(i) The kind of radical reform of curricula that became necessary in Eastern Germany in the wake of the collapse of the GDR and the unification with West Germany was not accomplished in one piece, but evolved through several stages.
(ii) In each period, the extent to which ideas for reform and change and the development of new curricula could be implemented was determined by the consensus that different mobilized social forces and the government were able to reach. The first phase of curricular reform saw much debate, but few actual measures of change, while the second phase saw much less debate, but encompassing state-sponsored change.
(iii) It is surprising that, despite the importance of curricular guidelines for the internal reform of schools, issues of instruction receive relatively less attention on the political stage of the new state, except for religion and moral education. This relatively low conflict intensity around issues of content and methods of instruction contrasts with the vehement clashes about the formal organizational structures (comprehensive vs. two- or three-tier system).
(iv) Under conditions of radical change and in the presence of extreme pressures for results, curriculum development proves to be feasible in a fraction of the time usually considered necessary. The swiftness of the process is facilitated when models and outside experts that know the models are available and when conflict can be held to a rather low level.

The First Phase of Curricular Change, 1989/90

It may be useful briefly to recall some of the salient GDR traditions from which curriculum reform departed in this phase:

(i) the old curriculum for all subjects had provided a detailed and very definitive set of instructions not only as to aims and content, but also to the instructional process itself;
(ii) the teacher had been bound by the curriculum plan and expected to implement it faithfully (*Lehrplantreue*); the space for instructional creativity was limited to the implementation of what had been centrally planned;
(iii) the systematic treatment of the subject had taken precedence over any kind of 'project learning';
(iv) instruction had been unequivocally teacher-centered;
(v) the class had been the sole and single unit of instruction, with very limited provision of internal or external differentiation;

(vi) subject matter and curricular goals had taken precedence over considerations of instructional organization and method;
(vii) the emphasis had throughout been on the 'scientific' quality of subject matter, leading effectively to a devaluation of experiential learning.

The 'scientific' principles of Marxism-Leninism, in which the political doctrine of the party was couched, were woven into the curricula of all subjects although some subjects were more affected than others. It was this kind of instructional setting that had shaped the perceptions and experiences of students, teachers, and parents who, in the fall of 1989, were confronted with the emergence of a substantially different educational and instructional philosophy.

The first period of curricular reform immediately preceded or followed the fall of the Berlin Wall on 9 November 1989 and ended with the dissolution of the GDR in October 1990. While most other segments of East German society underwent considerable disarray and disintegration in the wake of these dramatic events, the school proved to be a relatively stable system, where instruction continued as the institution sought to adjust to new conditions. The indeterminacy of the setting was seized by teachers and students as an opportunity for greater self-determination, interaction, and experimentation. While this new mood occasionally created friction within schools, it became a fertile ground for reform ideas, including ideas for new directions in curriculum development (*Deutsche Lehrerzeitung* 46/89 ff.; Bildungsreform, 1990; Gruner, 1990). Few of those, however, are reflected in actual reform measures.

The following reform measures were of particular significance for this phase:

(i) After the ouster on 2 November 1989, of Margot Honecker, who as the wife of the party Chairman had been Minister of Education for over a decade, the then still communist (SED) government announced the abolition of the subjects 'military education' (5 November) and 'citizenship education' (6 November) which had been carrying a particularly heavy ideological load; the periods that were thereby freed up were widely used for a variety of activities designed to help students (and teachers) cope with the new political situation (field trips, public discussions, etc.). A new subject 'societal education' (*Gesellschaftskunde*) was introduced, although initially without a curriculum and without trained teachers. Here as well, improvisation and imagination generated interesting new and open forms of instruction at the interface between school and society, but also caused a great deal of insecurity among teachers who had been used to a high degree of direction and prescription under the old order. There also were suspicions that some of the old *Staatsbürgerkunde* teachers merely continued to teach the old material under new labels (Berndt, 1990). To find substitutes for the now obsolete ideological content of GDR textbooks, many teachers relied more and more on Western textbooks and materials that were massively introduced to East German schools by enterprising West German publishers.

(ii) The Central Committee of the SED envisioned the formation of 'achievement classes' (*Leistungsklassen*) on 10 November, effective as early as the second semester of the 1989/90 school year. This was probably less an emulation of Western practices than a more general reaction to the lack of internal differentiation (especially in grades 9 and 10) in the GDR system. Particularly under the post-SED government, this increase in differentiation was accompanied by an opening of the college-prep track to a much larger percentage of students who were to be selected only on the basis of achievement.

(iii) Russian was 'dethroned' as the obligatory first foreign language in all GDR schools (13 November). It was to be replaced by Western languages, particularly English, for which there was strong demand among Eastern German students.

(iv) The school week was reduced from six to five days a week (18 November). This rather substantial reduction was bound to have curricular repercussions. Instruction in the natural sciences, a strong area of emphasis in GDR schools, was primarily affected.

(v) As part of the *ad hoc* adjustment of existing curricula to changing objectives and conditions, a dazzling array of new regulations was promulgated over the first six months of 1990. They touched, in varying degrees, on the curriculum in virtually all subjects, but left the basic structure of the curriculum, except for the points mentioned above, largely intact.

All of the decisions discussed in the preceding section formally originated in the Ministry of Education (of the then still existing GDR). In reality, however, many of them were the result of widespread pressure for reform by teachers, parents, students and the East German public at large, often articulating concerns and ideas that had already been discussed, albeit less openly, prior to the change in regimes. A case in point was a groundswell of opposition against retaining Russian — the language of the officially prescribed 'friends of the people of the GDR' — as the obligatory first foreign language. This, it may be recalled, was the period of the 'round tables' where the conduct of politics in the waning days of the GDR was largely a matter of almost continuous debates between representatives of different social groups with members of government agencies. The 'round tables for education' were particularly lively events, where the de-ideologizing of school and instruction, the need for greater differentiation, and for fostering the child's individual potential, and greater curricular and organizational flexibility were dominant and hotly debated issues.

The GDR Ministry of Education, under the leadership of its Deputy Minister, responded to this debate and to the need for change that it revealed by bringing into the Ministry a range of new personnel. This included some experienced curriculum specialists from the former Academy of Pedagogical Sciences, but also educational administrators from the local level as well as teachers who were known to be interested in educational reform. In one of the many ironies of this period, they worked towards the goal of reform alongside many of the hardliners left over from the era of Margot Honecker. As in many other realms of social and political life in the final days of the GDR, many of the new and innovative policy figures came into the public domain from their previous work in church organizations.

An important part of the nature of the education policy process was, as has already been described, the interaction between 'above' and 'below', with rather massive pressure from 'below' on a number of specific issues. For example, the demand for having no school on Saturdays, put forward regularly by teachers and parents for years, had been denied by Ms. Honecker right through the end of the old GDR regime. Now, with East Germans in large numbers using Saturdays for their shopping sprees in the West, students simply voted with their feet. While the early measures, doing away with the most unpopular features of the old system, were hastily implemented by a party desperately trying to stay in control of a wave of popular upheaval, the procedural model for most of the subsequent revisions involved more deliberation. It comprised the following steps:

(i) a phase of public 'problematizing' of an issue where representatives of social groups or the Ministry invited ideas and suggestions from teachers, parents, and other interested parties; typical were proposals for a civic education curriculum in November of 1989 (*Pädagogik* 12/89, p. 959 ff.) and for restructuring the relative weight of the different subjects in mid-1990 (*Deutsche Lehrer-Zeitung* 9/90, *Beilage*), both of which carried explicit invitations for public reaction;

(ii) the analysis and assessment of the reactions within the Ministry; for example, in the case of the revision of foreign language instruction in February of 1990, the Ministry's communication of the new rules specifically mentions the 'almost 500' written reactions received by the Ministry as an important input into the decision process (*Deutsche Lehrer-Zeitung* 35/90, p. 12);

(iii) the ratification and implementation of the new policy, much of which was cast in the language of 'recommendation' rather than 'direction'.

Participants in, and observers of, the policy and reform process of curriculum during this early and eventful phase agree that there was a remarkable degree of tolerance and compromise on general principles even where there was dissent on specifics, in a period that was otherwise characterized by a good deal of political disagreement. One should not forget, however, that the still-SED reform government was too weak to resist popular forces, that the latter were too fragmented to shape a new school with a unified program, and that the post-SED government, voted into office in March 1990, was more of a caretaker for the imminent all-German authorities rather than an active force of reform. Reform enthusiasm on all parts was increasingly affected by concerns over the impending accession of the GDR to the Federal Republic of (West) Germany and its implications for education and curriculum development (Schwerin, 1990, p. 73f.). The one domain where disagreements were so strong that compromise proved to be beyond reach was religious instruction (Tiefensee, 1990); in this area, the state had to reckon with a strong and independent political force, the Protestant church and, to a lesser degree, the Catholic church.

The Second Phase of Curricular Change, 1991–93

In macro-political terms, this phase began with the first state elections in the united Germany on 14 October 1990, just ten days after formal unification. In the state of Brandenburg — unlike the other four states where more 'conservative' governments headed by the Christian Democratic Union (CDU) were elected — the election brought a state government to power that is composed of a center-left coalition consisting of Social Democrats (SPD), Free Democrats (FDP) and *Bündnis 90* (which had emerged from the civil rights movements of the final days of the old GDR). The first Minister of Education in Brandenburg was Marianne Birthler of the *Bündnis 90*, who had earned a reputation as an advocate for democracy and human rights under the old SED regime and after the collapse of the regime had made it clear that she was determined to bring about a radical reform of the educational system. This determination became a major force in Brandenburg's educational policy, which aspired not only to getting rid of the command pedagogy of the old GDR system, but also to questioning some of the structures and mentalities prevailing in West German education.

Under the auspices of the Ministry of Education, the Land Brandenburg established in April 1991 the *Pädagogisches Landesinstitut Brandenburg* (PLIB) as a special agency for the initiation and coordination of curriculum development, corresponding programs for teacher in-service training, and for the monitoring of educational and curricular reform in the state.

The Brandenburg Educational Reform Act of May 1991 mandated major changes in the educational system as of the beginning of the 1991/92 school year; these changes had curricular implications, and required a substantial curriculum development effort prior to the start of the new school year in September. Given the time pressure, the Ministry concentrated on two tasks: new curricular frameworks had to replace the old syllabi in ten subjects which were either to be newly-introduced (for example, citizenship education) or 'ideologically' exposed (for example, German, history); all other subjects had to be reviewed as to absolutely necessary corrections, amendments, or clarifications of the old GDR curricula that were otherwise still valid.

Corresponding to the overall administrative consolidation in the new *Länder* of the united Germany, the cast of characters in this second phase is already more easily and clearly identifiable. It was composed essentially of:

(i) staff of the newly-created Ministry of Education, many of whom were either transferred or seconded from civil service positions in one of the West German *Länder* — typically North Rhine-Westphalia, which is traditionally a SPD-governed state and which had entered into a special partnership with Brandenburg for the purpose of building up the latter's system of state government;
(ii) teachers from Brandenburg and neighboring West Berlin, who had mostly volunteered for the task and who were presumably selected for their specific reform spirit;
(iii) 'technical experts', i.e., curriculum specialists from various agencies and institutions, mostly from West Germany[1]; and
(iv) members of the staff of PLIB who were often from the West as well.

As far as one can determine, the actors involved in this process insured a dominance of 'progressive' ideas for the new curricula. An attempt was made to balance the curriculum commissions, in which the actual rewriting was done, in terms of origin between educators from Brandenburg and those from West Germany, and in terms of background between curriculum specialists, government administrators, and teachers, with a number of participants fitting into two or all three of these categories. The composition of the commissions along these criteria varied, however, according to subject areas (see below).

This initial phase of curriculum development at the state level in Brandenburg was essentially a phase of transition between the spirited, but somewhat amorphous attempts at educational change during the year preceding unification and the establishment of the new *Länder* as functioning units of political and administrative organization. One organizational cornerstone, the construction of a coherent and comprehensive instructional concept and curricular framework for the new state educational system, was still a task lying ahead. The results of this interim phase allowed the educational system in Brandenburg to move into a substantially modified, but still not altogether revised incarnation by the beginning of the 1991/92 school year.

The school year 1991/92 in Brandenburg (and elsewhere in Eastern Germany) was in many ways an administrator's nightmare and a reformer's dream. New types and forms of schools had replaced the standard ten-year GDR school, and teachers, students and parents had great difficulty orienting themselves in a much more complex and confusing array of educational structures. The 'Unification Treaty' stipulated that Brandenburg, like the other Eastern German states, had to institute the Western three-tier structure in some form. The State Ministry was pressured to accept the institution of the college-preparatory *Gymnasium* and of the middle-track *Realschule*, but it also made good on some of its equity commitments by introducing the *Gesamtschule* or comprehensive school on a large scale, which had not fared very well as an educational innovation in an earlier reform phase in West Germany (Weiler, 1983).

In the turmoil attending these structural transitions and confusions, the question of content and curriculum — of the 'inner reform' of the school — had almost disappeared from sight. At the same time, periods of transition do open up possibilities for new concepts of learning and instruction; it was the task of the PLIB to reinforce this agenda by undertaking a rewriting of all curricular guidelines. In two cycles (February–May 1992, and October 1992–January 1993), a total of fifty-nine subject matter 'frameworks' were developed, including several for subjects that had no precedent in Eastern Germany (law, philosophy, psychology, education and economics). The principal point of anchorage of this effort was in a special coordinating committee at the PLIB, which worked closely with the curriculum officers in the Ministry of Education. This committee put together and supervised subject matter commissions, and composed a basic orientation paper which articulated educational principles for the new Brandenburg curricula (Pädagogisches Landesinstitut Brandenburg, 1992).

A set of guiding ideas was adopted after a good deal of dispute between East and West German participants about the degree of content versus problem orientation in learning and of openness versus prescriptiveness of the curricula. These guiding ideas ended up prefacing each and every set of curriculum frameworks, providing a common instructional concept that was to cut across and shape different subject areas and their curricula. The principal points of this document on 'standards of instructional planning' can be summarized as follows:

(i) an orientation towards the student as a point of departure for the instructional process;
(ii) a need for the curriculum to be oriented towards action, and to overcome the GDR legacy of purely cognitive, receptive, and reproductive learning;
(iii) the need to identify issues or problems around which the instructional process could be oriented, and which are of sufficient import that all subjects can participate in dealing with them;
(iv) special emphasis on the importance of 'exemplarity', i.e., on the instructional utility of well-chosen examples for illuminating a larger context;
(v) the linkage between the curriculum and scientific knowledge, with much greater emphasis on the methods of scientific work and less emphasis (compared to the GDR) on the acquisition of systematic disciplinary knowledge;
(vi) a careful weighing between the principle of openness for instructional experimentation and the constraints imposed by the federal mechanisms for recognizing school diplomas.

With this preface both preceding and shaping the curricular frameworks for the various subjects, a common 'progressive' frame of reference for guiding instructional practice was established even though the document reflects compromises between Eastern educational traditionalism and Western progressivism. The curricula developed for individual subjects reflect this frame of reference, but the way the compromise was achieved differed depending on the relationship of the subject to the GDR past, which in turn determined the composition of the curriculum commissions.

In the case of traditional subjects with little or no ideological connotations (for example, the natural sciences), the majority of the commission members were educators from Brandenburg, who were typically joined by one teacher or didactics specialist from West Germany in an advisory capacity. Where traditional, but ideologically sensitive subjects (such as German) were involved, the commissions usually ended up with a parity of East and West, ostensibly in order to correct for whatever one-sidedness the tradition of the subject in the GDR had suffered from. West Germans were as much as possible recruited from different West German states to avoid the preponderance of any one curriculum perspective. However, most of West Germans came from educationally 'progressive', left-of-center governed states.

In the commissions that worked on subjects for which there had been no precedent in East German schools (such as law or philosophy), West German educators and curriculum specialists were in the majority, and the representatives of Brandenburg were primarily responsible for making sure that the emerging curriculum was sufficiently cognizant of the conditions under which local teachers and students were operating. The commission in charge of the new 'moral education' subject (*Lebenskunde-Ethik-Religion*, or *LER*) was enlarged to allow the representation of the various groups that had claimed a stake in the outcome of this particular development, notably the churches.

As an illustration of how the Ministry's educational philosophy and political will has exerted its influence over the new curricula, we will take a brief look at a few subjects and at the kinds of conflict they have generated during this phase of comprehensive reform.

The framework commission for Chemistry (college-prep upper division), in its majority Eastern German, was originally headed by a professor from a local university who had in the past been instrumental in developing the GDR syllabi for Chemistry. Although verbally supportive of the 'progressive' agenda of the 'guiding ideas', he tended to favor traditional content-oriented approaches. While he, as an authority in his field, overshadowed the three Brandenburg teachers on the commission, he clashed with the sole West German member, a progressive teacher from West Berlin, who subsequently resigned. It was not until PLIB staff intervened and combined the chemistry commission with parts of the biology commission — which conducted its business in the 'right' reform spirit — that the chemistry commission produced the desired results.

No such difficulties were encountered in those commissions that were dominated by progressive educators from the West who duly produced the intended open and student-centered frameworks. For example, the commission for college-prep German submitted a curriculum that does not contain a literature canon, but limits itself to specifying selection criteria for teachers; in addition, in clear departure from the prescriptive GDR syllabus it leaves about a third of instruction time up to the planning discretion of local faculties.

The writing of the philosophy framework was in the hands of four Westerners, two from Hamburg and two from West Berlin. One Brandenburg teacher complemented the commission. Interestingly, a rival group of Western philosophers, disagreeing with the principles of the commission, demanded to be included. PLIB staff — the Director of the Institute being a professor of philosophy himself — decided to maintain the ideological cohesion of the commission and offered representatives of alternative approaches the opportunity of participating as outside evaluators.

It had been one of the early commitments of the new Brandenburg government to provide in its schools an opportunity for constructively coping with the collapse of the old (GDR) system of social norms and with the challenge of assessing and exploring new normative options. For this purpose, the introduction of a new subject — *Lebenskunde-Ethik-Religion* (LER) — was decided in June 1991 as an obligatory, interdenominational part of the secondary school curriculum beginning in grade 7. The subject does not have antecedents anywhere, but is newly-designed for Brandenburg. The subject matter to be covered in LER is as yet rather vague, but the basic idea is to find ways to address, and reflect upon, the students' own experiences, fears, hopes, and dilemmas, and place them in the context of the cultural, spiritual, and moral traditions that have shaped and continue to shape a modern pluralist society. In contrast to other subjects, LER was not to be defined by a definite subject matter or body of scientific knowledge (Kriesel, 1993).

This decision immediately ignited a major confrontation between the two Christian churches and the Land government over the threat that this new subject posed to the (constitutionally guaranteed) status of denominational religious instruction in public schools. Besides the point of principle, the new policy had financial implications for the churches in that denominational religious instruction assured the state's support for both the salaries and the training of teachers of religion.

The resolution of this crisis was ingenious, and not without precedent in German education policy. To defuse the controversy, the decision to introduce the new subject was transformed into an 'experiment' where a number of schools (one in each county of the Land) would try out the new subject in grades 7 and 8 for a trial period of three years[2]. This period would at the same time give the teachers an opportunity to develop, with the assistance of appropriate in-service programs, more of a formal curriculum on the basis of the general premises that were described above.

Curriculum Reform Between Assimilation and Differentiation

Except for the issue of religion and moral education where the churches as societal actors became involved, curriculum development in Brandenburg remained an internal affair among education professionals and Ministry officials. The Ministry in conjunction with the central curriculum institute (PLIB) was able to maintain a philosophical cohesion of the process without encountering much conflict. This resulted in the speedy production of curricula that are essentially in line with ideas of educational progressivism. The Ministry relied on much expertise and support from Western left-of-center governed states and from reform-minded teachers, Eastern as well as Western. Neither traditional GDR approaches (presumably still widely held among GDR educators) nor conservative Western approaches exerted much influence. A symbolic balance between Western and Eastern professionals, avoiding conflict by externalizing dissenting ideas, and introducing controversial issues as scientific experiments, combined with the thorough discreditation of the old curricula in the eyes of the public, all contributed to the swiftness of the reform process that was required by the void which the vanished GDR left behind.

The 'curricular frameworks' that emerged from this process, imperfect and preliminary as some of them still are, differ markedly not only from their own predecessors, but also in some aspects from curricular guidelines of other *Länder*. Their open design allows for student-centeredness, teachers' professional authority, and ideological pluralism.

Participation in the Brandenburg commissions has encouraged West German educators and didactics specialists to reopen in their own *Länder* the question of curriculum reform, particularly in the direction of integrated, cross-disciplinary, and multi-grade courses, the new 'moral education' (LER) experimental curriculum, and courses where Brandenburg has utilized some successful GDR lessons, notably in astronomy and generally in more vocational subjects (economics, technology, social work).

A remarkable and potentially seminal characteristic of the Brandenburg effort is the fact that curricula were designed for grade levels rather than school types (*Gymnasium, Gesamtschule*, etc.). This may facilitate the permeability of the system and students' mobility across different school types, at a time when teachers, parents, and students are preoccupied with understanding the differences among the new school types and begin to conceptualize learning in terms of the three-tier system.

The pressure of time, and especially the lack of a grace period between the development and the implementation of the new curricula, made it mandatory to establish from the start a close connection between curriculum development and teacher in-service training, and to involve members of the commissions in programs to familiarize teachers with the new frameworks. A major challenge lies ahead in the evaluation of this massive program of curricular innovation. Among the many questions to be answered by the ongoing evaluation, perhaps the most critical has to do with how teachers, whose personal and professional past was tied up with a very different curricular and instructional philosophy, cope with curricular guidelines that do not only outline new content, but are also based on the expectation of a very different way of dealing with both knowledge and students. Many teachers' expectations may be disappointed not so much by what the new curricula spell out, but by what they do not prescribe anymore.

Initially, this chapter had considered curriculum reform in the new *Länder* of Eastern Germany in terms of the dichotomy of 'assimilation' and 'differentiation'. In doing this, we suggested that one of the, and perhaps *the* most critical dimension of providing East German schools with a new instructional and curricular frame of reference was to reconcile the considerable pressure of homogenization that arose in the wake of East Germany's accession to the territory of the West German republic with the need and/or desire of East German educators, parents, and students for a certain degree of educational identity of their own, and for a measure of differentiation as far as both the ends and the means of the educational process is concerned.

The chapter has shown how one particular *Land* in Eastern Germany, Brandenburg, has tried to cope with this dilemma in developing a new set of curricular guidelines or frameworks for its schools within a little more than two years since the legal conclusion of German unity. The process began with the dramatic events of the fall of 1989 and was shaped in important ways by the innovative energies that were released by these events. In the span of less than a year, a reform agenda had developed that, while breaking radically with the educational past of the GDR, differentiated itself as clearly from the model of West Germany.

As that model became, as it were, the law of the land in October 1990, the ground rules for the process changed significantly, and the tension between 'assimilation' and 'differentiation' became much more real. The new *Länder* in Eastern Germany were faced with the awesome task of undoing decades of instructional practice and content and to lay the groundwork for a new educational system that would be functioning within the new, Western-dominated society without being totally absorbed or assimilated by it. Through two different phases of curriculum development, the state of Brandenburg has struggled with this challenge, relying on a variety of actors and a range of different procedural devices.

Even now, in the very early stages of the implementation of the new curricula, one can safely say that something *sui generis* has been achieved through this process, and that Brandenburg has resisted at least to some extent the temptation of adopting ready-made curricular prescriptions from elsewhere; the curricula in law and philosophy, and the experimental program in moral education (LER) are cases in point. The further development of this program, however, will continue to face the dilemma expressed earlier in this chapter: the social dynamics of the powerful West German presence in Eastern Germany will continue to militate in the direction of greater homogeneity and assimilation; the teachers will continue to have difficulties, although perhaps on a declining scale, with an instructional philosophy that is so much at variance with their own professional socialization; and the people of Eastern Germany will continue to be torn between the desire to have an educational system in which they recognize themselves and their peculiar situation, and the temptation to emulate their 'successful' brothers and sisters in the West. The jury is still out.

Notes

1. The most important role was played by the *Landesinstitut für Schule und Weiterbildung* in Soest, a kind of educational R&D center for the state of North Rhine-Westphalia.
2. There are a number of precedents for this kind of creative conflict management in education policy. The best known perhaps is the conflict over the introduction of comprehensive secondary schools (Gesamtschulen) in the Federal Republic of (West) Germany in the late 1960s and early 1970s. When the polarization over this issue made it impossible to proceed with the full-fledged introduction of the new type of schools, a number of the new comprehensive schools were introduced on an experimental basis, thereby putting off a decision on the matter until more evidence was available and, hopefully, animosities had cooled down (see Weiler, 1983 and 1989).

Chapter 4

Teachers and the Democratization of Schools

Studying Democratic Schools

In Guttmann's (1987) model of a democratic school, the various participants in the educational endeavor share the authority to control what happens in schools. States are the legitimate representatives of common political will and culture, communities express their cultural identities, parents pursue their right to educate their child, educators possess authority to run schools with professional expertise and to dispense a pluralist curriculum, and students enjoy personal integrity and the space to participate. Boundaries between authority domains may shift, but it is essential for democratic schools that one domain not rule to the exclusion of all others. In addition, certain non-discriminatory and distributive principles apply as democratic universals that cannot be overruled by democratic control.

Democratic schools are an important and special case of institutions that need to come to life in order to sustain a successful transition from authoritarian rule (O'Donnell and Schmitter, 1986) and to form a democratic political culture. Almond and Verba (1963) deal with this critical issue in their classical study on 'civic culture'. According to their 1959 findings, democracy fares best when it is congruent with a political culture that balances citizens' roles as subjects with participant role orientations. Citizens derive their sense of political participation from direct experiences in the political realm as well as from socialization processes in family, school and other institutions. Post-war West Germany, overcoming the disaster of authoritarian Nazi rule, initially lacked participatory elements in the culture of politics, family and schools that were more prevalent in the established Anglo-Saxon democracies. Western liberal-democratic institutions, imposed on the country by the allied powers from above, had not taken firm roots yet. A similar situation may obtain now in the Eastern part of the country due to the long absence of a democratic culture and of democratic structures in the experience of East Germans.

Teachers are potentially eminent role models in the emerging democratic state. Whether they will actually play this part will depend to a large degree on their own particular experience of active participation and passive allegiance as citizens and servants of the new state. A third element needs to be considered. Autonomy and privacy loom large in societies that embark on a process of liberalization from obligatory participation and collective action, previously organized under the regiment of socialist mass mobilization.

Taking cues from the literature on democratic schools and political culture, we sought to find out how the relationships among school site actors change, how authorities exert control over schools in this change, and to what degree educators (i.e., teachers and principals) are participants in this process. We look at this process through the lens of one set of actors, teachers and principals at school sites. Staying with this bottom-up approach of the 'teacher's-eye perspective' on educational change (Little and McLaughlin, 1993), we believe that for an adequate understanding of an issue, such as the democratization of school site relationships, we need to refer back to the core of teachers' work, the interdependence among teachers, students, and content in classroom and school contexts. Our data strongly bear out this assumption, even for conditions of large-scale societal change.

Thus, the process of democratizing schools comes into view in its 'meaning' (Fullan, 1991) for educators. Meaning is uncovered through actors' testimonies and observations of behavior. In this chapter, we present data gathered during a six months' stay in Eastern Germany in 1991 and 1992. We interviewed about 100 educators face-to-face in two states, Brandenburg and Thüringen. Our informants were Ministry of Education and county officials, principals and teachers. We concentrated on eight schools, four in each state. College-preparatory and vocation-oriented school types are evenly represented. The schools are located in five different counties. In these schools we observed about forty lessons in various subjects. In addition, we were observers at several training retreats for principals, large meetings with the ministers of education, and group discussions. We collected written records on statutes, regulations, and other pertinent material. In addition, we took the opportunity to talk to a number of students and classes.

Rather than starting from policies of democratization and identifying their effects on schools, we proceeded indirectly. In an open query we started from the broader experience of East German teachers' work lives and tried to comprehend significance and strength of particular issues that have to do with democratization and were embedded in that experience. The format of the interviews was fairly open. It basically consisted of two parts. To gain a more broad-based idea of an educator's reality, we would ask a principal or teacher to highlight changes that were due to the recent political transformation ('*Wende*') and that had a great impact on their work at school, assuming that 'shift of system' or 'democracy' would be among them. If it had not already happened, we would then direct the informant to talk about issues concerning democratization: changed relationships at school sites, their attitude towards the new state, and their role in the change process. In this way, we gave our informants the opportunity for at least part of the interview to direct us to their concerns rather than immediately answering our specific research question. The open-ended inquiry format yielded data that were subsequently organized according to patterns that emerged from the data and were relevant to our topic (Mostyn, 1985). These patterns were grouped into themes that became the building blocks of this presentation. Within these themes we will highlight prevailing sentiments and point out contrasting versions wherever we encountered them with sufficient consistency and in large enough numbers, or whenever they articulated especially insightful revelations. The reliability of the study is strengthened by identifying elements that occur with sufficient repetition; generally, those will be reported.

The openness of our query did not mean, however, that we approached educators with a blank slate. We were and are mindful of the broader historical and social context and of existing policy mechanisms that may affect school life. For our study of democratization, as one may recall from a previous chapter, we have to take into account the historical experience of a short-term grassroots upheaval whose effect on schools is nonetheless unclear, and the imposition of an institutional shell that may constrain school site actors as much as it may enable them to cultivate democracy.

From the state governments' perspective the democratization of schools is at this point mainly a legal affair. In some fashion, the school reform acts stipulate the right of legal guardians to educate their child (cf. Thüringer Kultusministerium, 1991a, para. 2.2), the individual responsibility of teachers as classroom instructors (*ibid*, para. 11.2), the dispensation of pluralist world views (Ministerium für Bildung, Jugend und Sport, 1991, para. 2), shared decision-making for parents, students, and teachers at school sites (Thüringer Kultusministerium, 1991a, paras. 21–4), students' freedom of speech and the right to file grievances (Thüringer Kultusministerium, 1991b, paras. 4.2 and 5.1), parents' right to sue the school (*ibid*, para. 22.1). These are some of the more important legal principles of democratic schools that mark a departure from previous GDR practices. These are complemented by the citizens' right to vote as well as their ability to organize politically.

There is disagreement on many issues among this large group of educators that we came in contact with. However, we were able to identify eight themes relating to issues that are relevant for the process of democratization and that are raised consistently, mostly during the open questioning part of the interviews. Change in the educators' role towards parents and students is captured by the themes of authority, proximity and meritocracy; changes in the educators' professional role is grasped through the themes of competence and ambiguity; and changes in the political role of teachers and principals are grouped under the themes of legitimacy, subordination, and participation. Some of these themes refer to democratization processes in an indirect way. They receive privileged attention in this chapter due to the vigor with which they were presented in the interviews by comparison to less strongly voiced issues (e.g., governance, association, etc.) that may be more directly related to democratic procedures in schools.

Teachers, Students and Parents

The most profound change that was mentioned repeatedly and with great intensity in the interviews was a shift in the way students and parents nowadays relate to teachers. Reconstructing the GDR's past from the vantage point of present-day educators, teachers seem to have enjoyed a relatively unchallenged position of authority towards parents and students as long as the former performed their work according to state and party guidelines. The socialist school had primacy over the family in matters of education. Teachers were responsible for the success and failure of their wards in school and life. The evaluation of a teacher could make or break a student's career. Teachers coined the phrase: 'The teachers delivered (*Die Lehrer haben gemacht*)'. According to teachers' accounts, unless parents were in high places they rarely were able to overrule the school's decision. Cases of discrimination against religious students, for example, are pointed to in a few interviews, but for the most part, teachers feel they took a burden off parents' shoulders, and parents went along with it. Teachers were granted the moral authority by the state to decide for students and parents; they 'knew best' what was good for the student.

If a student did not comply with the rules or acted up in class, a 'well-oiled machine' — in the words of a principal — was set in motion that backed the teacher's authority. A teacher could activate the parent group for the student's 'class collective' that intervened in the private affairs of all students of the collective. Each class collective was adopted by a 'brigade', a collective of workers from a neighboring company, that could be called in 'to straighten the student out'. None of this is in place anymore: the ties to the world of work are cut now that the companies are private entities; and active parents can no longer be counted on as automatic allies, nor can they concern themselves with other people's children anymore.

This is not to say that teachers during GDR times did not encounter discipline problems. Some teachers report that in certain neighborhoods — particularly the old sections of town — things could be tough even then.

But the overwhelming majority of teachers interviewed complain about a turn to the worse after 1989. Some seem helpless, others shocked, many bitter. The phrase one frequently hears, especially in the lower-track schools, is that of 'misunderstood freedom' (falsch verstandene Freiheit). The sentiment is that after the pressure of the past regime has been lifted, students believe everything is permitted now and 'don't know their boundaries anymore'. Teachers find dialogue with their students difficult because the latter are said to be either interested in being merely disruptive or argue their point with great intolerance. In our observations, we saw both students and teachers being reticent, if not shy, to get involved in open discussions, but once a certain threshold was crossed one's opinion was presented with forceful imposition on another's view.

A few exceptions notwithstanding, even teachers in the college preparatory tracks, a minority of whom feel more positive about the loosening of discipline standards, are not sure about the eventual outcome of this development. Students, it seems, have become incalculable, giving in to the new stimuli of fashion, media, Western youth culture, and right-wing rebellion.

The state and school administration, once backing up the school's authority, has supposedly tilted in favor of students and parents. Three measures are frequently highlighted in teachers' accounts: (i) the abolition of citizenship grades — a decision which, due to their previously precarious usage, is not approved by most educators in the study; (ii) the introduction of legal principles of due process that in the eyes of many informants amount to poorly understood bureaucratic procedures that hinder pedagogical measures and unduly increase the rights of students and parents; and (iii) giving parents a large — in Brandenburg the final — say over a student's school career (for example, in the admission to or the removal from the college-preparatory Gymnasium). The latitude of this last measure is still contested in the courts in Thüringen. While the first two measures blunt teachers' disciplinary action, the third one questions the school's professional domain of evaluating student performance and assigning school careers accordingly. It is particularly resented by college-preparatory Gymnasium teachers and principals who deal with parents that are more likely to exercise their rights, but many lower-track teachers concur with this feeling. For lower-track school principals and teachers it is threatening that parents now have the right to shop for a school, and their schools face a hard selling job as a result.

Comments such as: 'As a teacher, one stood above the parents, now it's the other way around', — 'Parents wouldn't have dared before...', — 'Parents have the primacy now, but they need to fill it out', are symptomatic of a crumbling hierarchical relationship between teachers and parents, a process that is emotionally charged for many East German teachers.

In two schools, there was some evidence of a new relationship being forged with parents. These schools owed their existence or status to parents' political lobbying directed against state or local policies. Educators in these schools, more so than in others, put great emphasis on a parent-teacher partnership for the well-being of the school.

The theme of diminished authority is related to the theme of diminished familiarity or proximity. East German polytechnical schools, as reconstructed from teachers' responses, were small (400 students) neighborhood schools organized around stable heterogeneous core groups of students ('class collectives') in which students remained throughout their ten-year school career from grade 1 to grade 10. Teachers would get to know their students as little kids and would accompany them until they were ready to go to work. As mentioned before, ties between the community and the school were strong. As a manifestation of their commitment to the socialist society, teachers were required to spend after-school hours with their students, directing hobbies, sports, social activities, trips, etc., within the framework of the state youth organization: the so-called 'FDJ-Nachmittage'. In addition, visits at the students' homes were mandatory.

Many teachers feel that during GDR times they knew their students well, were close to them, and bonded with them. Thus, in many teachers' views, their authority was not only based on discipline, but also on paternal or maternal closeness. Stories abound of teachers cherishing the close contact and the less formal activities with young people in those days. With the demise of the party regime, the state youth organization was banned from schools which in effect led to the dismantling of the structure for most after-school activities; home visits, frowned upon as control visits, were discouraged by the new authorities; and neighborhood schools for all children were dissolved. Some educators voice their relief at being rid of these extra-curricular requirements, some reject them for the coercion involved, many more are undecided on the subject. The overwhelming majority, however, does express a sense of loss — almost mourning — of family at school. (Incidentally, we found students in the higher grades sharing that feeling.) Particularly at the lower-track schools, teachers miss the supportive role of parents.

There are two groups of educators that assess the theme of proximity to clients in rather different ways: the critics of authoritarianism and the advocates of achievement.

(i) Although a larger number of the ones that miss the old school family concede that students, characterized as compliant and gullible, were sometimes taught with pressure and 'treated rough', only a very small group, five teachers from all types of schools in our sample, is vociferously critical about the authoritarian structure of the relationship with clients. A principal from Thüringen puts it this way:

> Students and parents have never told us the truth. How could we have known then? Closeness was a fraud (*Trugschluß*). Without freedom of speech, there can be no closeness.

As a remedy, some teachers have turned to psychology and try to create a healthier bond with students, like one teacher who previously was a committed party activist and has now directed her zeal to understanding all those human elements that were blanked out under socialism. The principal quoted above, however, advocates more distance as a prerequisite for open communication.

(ii) Here, he is in agreement with the advocates of meritocracy. This group holds that for teachers to enforce strict academic performance standards they have to give up the doting ('*Glucken*') over students that was common in the GDR. The 'doting' resulted from a great concern of authorities and teachers over student failure. By contrast, most educators now stress the importance of student achievement and advancement based on it, a preoccupation that seems to supersede other political, social, and pedagogical goals of schools. Thus in the eyes of many, the idea of tracking has begun to look like an attractive alternative to the GDR schools.

During our school visits, principals would without fail show us the newly redecorated rooms in their buildings. East German classrooms, even hallways, are usually decked out with flower-patterned wallpaper; the windows are adorned by drapes, curtains and flower pots, giving classrooms the feel of living rooms. The new rooms, redone by students, teachers, or sometimes by the principal himself, look differently: the drapes are gone in many instances, and the walls are painted in bright white; the feel is business-like.

Are relationships between educators and students and parents becoming more democratic? From the point of view of a large group of educators this is not the issue. Teachers recognize that the new Western legal framework has given citizens, parents, and students a greater voice in schools and that the new political and cultural experience of parents and students has created a greater willingness on their part to exercise that voice and assert themselves towards teachers. But teachers for the most part register this process as a loss of authority, greater discipline problems, and a hindrance to good practice.

It must, indeed, be difficult to differentiate between parents' and students' legitimate concern for respect and participation and their acting-out of dissatisfaction, of disorientation, and — in the case of some students — of outright hooliganism. Thus, a decrease of their authority that was borrowed from and dependent upon a state and party beyond the reach of democratic control, is a double-edged sword for teachers.

While small neighborhood schools, the interlocking of school, free-time, family, community and the state economy, the absence of legal formality and the discouragement of segregating failure fostered a paternalistic relationship between teachers and clients, the new institutional order has led to a loosening of control. It has separated the various spheres of an individual's life. A new distance between teachers and students has emerged that gives room for the individual development of students, but also creates demands for individual responsibility of students to chart their own successful career or else bear the consequences of failure. Thus the liberalization of schools is accompanied by increased anonymity and less caring.

Teachers and Their Profession

The data suggest that the professional competence of a great many educators is challenged as they grapple with an overload of educational innovations, new policies, new ambiguities, and new cultural phenomena in society, schools, and classrooms. Several areas that affect competence are highlighted by the interviews with teachers and principals.

New Subject Matter

(i) New state curricula, fashioned after Western models, have been handed down by the authorities, and new textbooks furnished by Western publishing companies have been distributed. Teachers of all subjects report initial great confusion and a period of major adjustment when the stock of lesson plans that had provided safe grounds for practitioners during GDR times had to be discarded or at least redone to fit the new demands. Teachers with many years of experience point out that they can barely keep up with what pupils could read independently in the new textbooks.

(ii) Teachers of some subjects (for example, history, German) report problems of coping with an enlarged spectrum of theories and teaching material, previously unknown or forbidden to them, that is to be presented in class.

(iii) Instruction in some subjects was discontinued (for example, citizen education), greatly reduced (for example, Russian) or deemphasized (for example, science), new subjects are included in the schedule (for example, ethics) or greatly expanded (for example, English), making it necessary for a greater number of teachers to seek retraining in a new subject if they want to retain their position.

(iv) The expansion of the number of students reaching twelfth or thirteenth grade from what used to be about 10 per cent (GDR) to more than 30 per cent now has required many teachers to teach in unfamiliar grades — particularly higher ones that are taught a more demanding curriculum. One Gymnasium principal points out that 'proving oneself in front of the class as knowledgeable in one's subject area' has been a major preoccupation of teachers at his school; teachers concur.

(v) Fitting Eastern public employees into the structure of the West German civil service regulations has created certification problems for a number of teachers whose formal GDR qualifications are not deemed adequate for their current jobs anymore. These teachers, as well, are forced into retraining.

Achieving or improving subject matter competence, then, consumes a large amount of practitioners' time and energy. Many teachers mention a much higher workload due to increased preparation time and retraining. Subject matter appears to be of heightened concern in college preparatory schools. The number of teachers either voicing the need for brushing up on their subject knowledge or actually being involved in various retraining schemes is tremendous. A principal in one comprehensive school in Brandenburg, located in the rural vicinity of a metropolitan area, reports that fifteen out of thirty-five teachers are enrolled in extensive recertification courses at universities. In schools with less access to facilities, staff development has a lower profile, though awareness of a need for it seems high there as well.

New Technology of Teaching

The new state-induced technology of teaching is characterized by increasing ambiguity and openness where there used to be clarity and uniformity. There was one curriculum and one textbook that applied to almost all students and teachers in the GDR. The curriculum was detailed enough to determine single lessons. Model lesson plans in conjunction with textbooks guided the teacher in the prescribed direction. According to many interviews, teachers felt accountable to principals and mentor teachers to be at the right place in the curriculum when visited, though some teachers downplay this aspect. Such an intricately interwoven curriculum is not altered easily so that after a number of years on the job routine set in. Teachers 'knew their lessons'. — 'After a while nothing new happened anymore. That was it.'

Now, the unified curriculum is in tatters. First came the new Western textbooks that present content more based on principles of exemplary learning rather than on logical structure or chronology. Teachers could select from many books that were promoted by Western sales representatives without really knowing on what basis since the new curriculum was not in place yet. The new curricula that came later provided mere guidelines as to the general topics that need to be covered.

Reactions to this development are mixed. On one hand, teachers greet the new openness. A large number of teachers from all school types find teaching under the new circumstances generally more interesting. They name as advantages increased possibilities to allow for one's own personal interest in lesson planning, more creativity, and more flexibility in tailoring lessons to students' needs. Particularly teachers in arts and humanities cherish the new freedom of expression. On the other hand, teachers complain that the curricula are too 'inaccurate' and that curricula and textbook 'don't fit'. One teacher in Thüringen relates:

> We got our textbooks from Rhineland-Palatine, our in-service classes from Hessen, and our curriculum from Bavaria. It doesn't work.

Teachers report insecurity on what to teach, always being on the look-out for supplementary material (and in line for the newly-acquired copy machines) and ending up designing their individual curriculum, a quite unusual digression from the past.

This has the undesirable result, in the eyes of many, that the previous uniformity of the school is lost. Divergent content is taught in parallel classes, and grading standards become arbitrary. Collegiality is seen as a remedy against this drifting-apart. A lively collegiality — acting collectively — has a strong tradition in the GDR schools, according to teachers. But it was as much a means of mutual help as a vehicle of enforcing strong group norms. In some interviews, when educators talk of collegiality or the lack thereof, they seem to have this latter function in mind: 'The uniformly acting faculty remains our principle.'

One strategy of handling all this confusion and ambiguity is simply to jettison the overtly political components of the old curriculum and rely on the routine structure of the old lesson plans — politically cleansed — as the backbone and guiding light through the sea of changes. Although the old curricula, textbooks, and lesson plans are not official documents anymore and are banned from public view, they seem to be still in use in private, gone underground as it were. Some teachers and principals state openly that not much has changed in their curricula — words, but not actual content. Here again, the less ideological subjects are overrepresented.

Classroom Management

Handling classroom management and methods of successful lesson delivery is another challenge for teachers' competence, particularly in lower-track schools. While discipline standards have reportedly deteriorated in all schools visited, only the concentration of low achieving and less compliant students in the lower-track schools seems to have rendered the traditional methods unworkable. Although this point was raised by some Gymnasium teachers as well, more than half the educators interviewed in the Brandenburg comprehensive schools (mainly lower track) and almost as many in the Thüringen lower-track schools believe they need to learn new methods.

For the majority, helplessness abounds as to what skills will provide the remedy. A few comments point in the direction of a more open, student centered pedagogy: 'We were too content-centered. — Motivation is now key in instruction.' Others call for trained psychologists and counsellors at school or believe that a solution could be found in training teachers in a specific lower-track pedagogy that has been promised to them by some Western consultants.

New Laws and Directives

Teachers, and especially principals, cope with a flood of new laws and directives that involve norms of privacy, due process, etc., with which they are unfamiliar and which introduce a degree of behavior formalization they are unaccustomed to — although principals who are well connected with local governments take a more relaxed stand. One principal assumes — falsely — that schools cannot even report child abuse cases anymore. On a more mundane level, insurance liability has added an element of uncertainty to field trips that did not exist before. Teachers from several schools told me they were advised to keep their pay stubs hidden from colleagues. Parents' right to sue has forced teachers and principals to create written records and to follow a legally prescribed step-by-step course of action which teachers do not know.

'All this bureaucratic red tape', in the eyes of informants, has been imposed on the schools for the sake of a legal system that somehow holds together and seems to make sense if one looks West, but that nevertheless is cumbersome and alien to the professional and everyday experience of many Easterners. Some educators declare themselves incompetent judging certain legal provisions or policies since they feel they lack an understanding of the system as a whole. The lack of legal competence is especially disquieting for a group of public servants that are strongly socialized into complying with the ways of state authorities. 'We (Easterners) didn't know this. — We didn't have this here. — Our people are so unenlightened. —' are frequently heard phrases uttered with an apologetic demeanor.

Seeking New Sources of Competence

Although many teachers' professional competence seems challenged in legal and pedagogical matters, this is not to say that they feel incompetent as such. Insecurities notwithstanding, teachers are perceptibly in the process of reasserting themselves. The 'lost school year' of 1989/90, as some teachers referred to it, when so many things turned upside down and the old system dissolved, had been endured, and a new order is taking shape in schools, even though the broad contours of that order evolved without the input of most teachers. But the reassertion of competence betrays a defensive posture.

Prominent sources of competence that are revealed in the interviews are: relying on the solid grounds of one's subject or academic discipline and comparing oneself with the West. The old GDR curricula in all subjects were highly politicized, and a clear stand in favor of 'real socialism' was weaved through all subject matter. How did teachers deal with the end of the official socialist ideology?

> I told my students that what I had taught them was not history, but what they told us history was. I told them what I was taught myself, and I believed it. But it looks different now.

This teacher is clearly an exception in our study. In the Math and Sciences Department, we would often receive the answer: 'Math is math/chemistry is chemistry/ . . . It has nothing to do with the political system.' or: 'In polytechnical instruction (vocational education) we were mostly concerned with the technical side of things. They left us alone with politics.' The few teachers of German with whom we broached the topic speak of an enlarged body of literature, but not of a different approach.

Teachers from all school types claim that their old GDR textbooks were more systematic and more scientific. Observed lessons in biology and German brimmed with abstract concepts and complex words. Teachers later on commented with pride that they instructed on a scientific level. After a literature lesson on Tolstoy, the teacher was asked whether the political orientation of her lesson had changed from GDR times to now. Her reply: 'Oh, that wasn't political, those were our learning objectives then.' Among teachers a tendency is observable to reconstruct their past political role in technical terms. What constitutes the solid grounds of one's subject is said to be factual knowledge, measurable skills, and scientific expertise — elements, as we saw in a previous chapter, that are not new to East German educators, but serve a different function now.

Comparison with the West is another strategy of sustaining a sense of competence. At least three-quarters of the study participants had the opportunity to visit schools in the West, some with frequency. The two phrases being heard repeatedly during school visits were: 'In math/ science/ German/ ... we look good by comparison with the West —' or more generally: 'We don't need to hide behind the West.' It is doubtful that the frequency of these incantations is due to the fact that the interviewers come from the West. They were uttered too spontaneously for that.

In stressing the importance of being as good as the West, East German teachers acknowledge or imply that the West is the yardstick or the model by which one's own competence, skill, or accomplishment is measured. When asked what makes them equal to their Western colleagues, teachers tend to point to their academic standards in class and their students' achievement expressed in measurable skills — skills that are politically neutral, that is. In the natural sciences it is the amount of scientific content being covered. Teachers of German stress spelling and grammar. A few teachers, mainly in the humanities, however, describe with admiration lessons that they observed in the West during which students were very open with the teacher and true feelings were shared. Although discipline is a problem in East German schools, West German teachers are deemed even worse off in this regard. In a few in-depth interviews, teachers admit feeling shame, inferiority, intimidation, and awe towards the West. But these feelings are attached to either extra-school spheres, such as the economy, or when related to education, to personality traits rather than learning output: 'We know as much as they (Westerners) do, but they can sell it better.'

Yet, when teachers envision staff development cognitive schemes take precedent: knowing a new subject or what is new in one's subject, knowing new methods and new laws is of primary interest for practitioners. In these domains, teachers' eagerness to learn seems abundant. Interviews with staff developers at the state institutes for in-service training corroborate this finding. One of the week-long retreats for principals that one of the authors attended was facilitated by psychologists who centered their course on group dynamics. Most of the twenty or so principals from all over the state rejected the course as useless — they were not learning anything — and rebelled against it almost to the end when many of them began to see the rewards in such an approach.

How does the educators' professional competence impinge on the process of democratizing Eastern German schools? The issue is central for three reasons: (i) it cuts to the core of teachers' motivation and their capacity to change; without the feeling of being in command of one's subject and its methods, teachers will not overcome their present defensiveness; (ii) competent teachers will be able to fill the new openness and freedom of the curriculum with experiment and a pedagogy that meets the needs of students demanding more voice; (iii) due to their limited political role and their decreasing moral authority, it is the one area where teachers can establish new professional authority.

Teachers and Politics

'You can't blame teachers for the criminal aspects of the system that is gone now, but this is what happened after the "Wende".' The person who made this comment is an educator who reportedly never had great sympathies for the socialist system, kept his distance from the communist party, and is an elected county supervisor. Teachers feel unfairly singled out, treated as scapegoats for the blunders of the communist state, defamed as Reds by society. The old socialist teaching force, as a group, now has a serious problem of legitimacy which stems from the precarious political role it played in the service of party and state. The point should be stressed that this does not amount to a summary verdict of individual teachers. For example, we encountered a number of principals and former teachers who, after unification, were elected into office by the communities in which they taught.

While most informants are silent on their past role, some feel free, others even feel the urge to talk about it. It seems painful for most of them. There are those that stress their detachment from the party, some of them relish in telling stories about run-ins with party authorities and secret service, incidents that were often minor, but seem to have had serious repercussions for their professional advancement. Then there are those that hint at socialist convictions and party activity when they were younger and are now bitterly disappointed about the failure of their ideals. The majority minimizes the significance of their past, as the following ensemble of frequent comments suggests:

> You could not be a revolutionary and a teacher at the same time. — Teachers were no heroes. — We are all guilty in some ways. — We didn't know... — We as teachers were under tight surveillance. — Politics was forced upon us, but one could circumvent it to a certain degree.

Most of these respondents may agree with the opinion of this Gymnasium principal:

> Somehow we, burned children, need to come to terms with our curious past. But it is still too early. At the moment we leave it alone.

Rather than evaluating the past political role of their profession and finding new acceptance in the process, many teachers justify themselves and their work by using certain elements — now familiar to the reader — that promise to compensate for whatever political flaws their biography may have had:

— their academic knowledge and subject matter competence in its ideologically neutral, a-political form (i.e., technical knowledge);
— their job performance as being equal to the West;
— their potential contribution to economic development by stressing student achievement;
— their proximity to and care for students that contrast with the supposed 'lesson deliverer' type (*Stundengeber*) of the West — a point somewhat inconsistent with the meritocratic orientation.

In light of these strategies, it is not surprising that the overwhelming number of leaders in the educational system from principals all the way up to (Eastern) ministry officials who participated in the study are either former math, science, physical education, or shop teachers, apart from teachers affiliated with the church.

Since so many teachers have left unexamined their past political role as educators for the socialist state, their role of serving the new democratic state or the democratic system can only develop haltingly. It does not come as a surprise, then, that the issue of democracy is not featured prominently in the interviews. This may partly be due to the open interview guideline that did not elicit explicit statements on democracy per se. But on the other hand, the query was very open, and yielded even without direct prompting many responses on 'strong' topics such as discipline and even the past.

There are some teachers in the study that express having 'yearned for democracy'. Often they are the ones that criticize teachers for their authoritarianism in classrooms. Some teachers in this relatively small group voice having been oppressed. Among them are Christian teachers that had to hide their convictions, literature teachers that could not dare teach the books they liked most, nor conduct an open discussion in class for fear a student would say something out of order, foreign language teachers who taught 'second hand' because they could not travel, or art teachers who had the daunting task of channelling all creative energy of their students into the prescribed artistic tracks.

Not one person in the study expresses the wish of having the old GDR back. But one does encounter skepticism towards the new democracy, as these few comments reveal:

> There is no freedom of speech now, either. — We thought injustice had stopped. — Democracy: every man for himself. — There is no democracy in a Western factory either.

To what extent the comments represent the sentiments of study participants is difficult to say from the data collected. The data, though, are better on teachers evaluating their direct experience with democracy in the transformation of schools.

There is a smaller group of educators in each state that, according to the interviews, are or had been active participants in the recent reform of the educational system at some time in the process. They tell of hopes, stimulation, and activity during the transition period 1989/90 when educational policy was made at the local level and schools were left to chart their own course. 'We wanted to create something of our own', finds broad consent among these educators.

But many of them are disillusioned now. When the new system was put together by the new state authorities, they felt they were left out: 'Nobody has asked us. They levelled everything we had. (*Bei uns wurde alles platt gewalzt*).' They complain that the Eastern school system has become 'a copy of the West' without regard to Eastern traditions and needs. Particularly in the lower-track schools in both states we found teachers that report having written plans and suggestions on school development without getting a response from authorities. These teachers, disagreeing with recent developments as well as with the governance style of the new authorities, have withdrawn from the reform process. It is not quite clear to what degree they had become active before. It seems that they did not actually join the political fray, but rather expected to be heard by the authorities out of concern for their own schools.

By contrast, a relatively small group is still optimistic and willing to actively participate. Among them are all the principals in the study and some teachers that have taken over official functions or career positions (for example, as members of curriculum commissions, mentors, etc.). Disagreements about details notwithstanding, this group of respondents is on the whole in active support of the new system. Few in the study are involved in political work for professional associations whose presence is not felt much at any of the eight schools that were visited.

The prevailing attitude among teachers, however, is compliance and subordination whether one agrees or disagrees with the decisions made higher up. There is not an incidence of visible resistance against policies on the part of teachers in this study that was not backed up by outside support of either community, local government, or state government. Teachers try to follow the guidelines that are handed down to them by the authorities even if some of the measures may not make sense to them. When asked why this is so, I found teachers frequently answering with a shrug, 'We GDR teachers are used to obey.' Other comments point in the same direction: 'We've always done what was demanded of us from above.' Some say they are afraid of attracting negative attention for fear of losing their jobs. Schools had just gone through a wave of lay-offs in one of the states, Thüringen, but insecurity was tangible in the other state as well. Some principals complain that teachers have a tendency to ask permission for too many things.

A good illustration is provided by the process of reassigning teachers of a given district to the new schools that were created with the reorganization of the socialist unitary school into tracked school types. All personnel had to be reassigned to redesignated schools. Teachers could submit a wish list stating the school type in which they wanted to continue their career. They then heard of their new assignment a couple of weeks before the beginning of the school year. Almost none of the teachers knew the actual procedure being followed, some guessed it was done by lottery, others thought it was political or decided on the whims of administrators. Some thought it might be qualification, but weren't sure. For most teachers, the process was arbitrary although they were glad when it came out according to their wishes. They took it as a stroke of fate, but seem to acquiesce to it regardless of outcome.

A seasoned teacher working at a lower-track school in Brandenburg wraps up the prevailing mood quite well:

> The question of power is resolved (*die Machtfrage ist geklärt*) and we have acted according to the demands from above, as we have done during GDR times. The new school system was decided by the politicians. They made us reapply and left us alone with our worries about our means of livelihood. We had to keep our mouths shut. We received some information from the principal about the new system, and then we continued muddling along.

With the exception of the few active functionaries of the new system, teachers seem largely to have withdrawn from the big questions of society and system. Instead they focus their energies on the domain where they are left to muddle along: their own subject areas and classrooms where it is in their discretion to plan and dispense lessons. While reticent towards system issues and insecure about client relationships, many teachers act in their subjects like pioneers. This orientation reverberates with the view of officials from both states that concede the realm of actual instruction to educators or, in other words, put it squarely on educators' shoulders.

The most active functionaries of the new system in this study are principals and local superintendents. In both counties that were studied in more depth, local superintendents had a high profile in local school affairs during the period of upheaval. Some had been active dissidents in the opposition while the party was still in power. Others had connections to the non-socialist satellite parties that existed in the GDR. Principals (and a few active teachers) are the ones that maintain links between their schools and the communities in which there was political activism around school issues. In one county, the three principals interviewed hold a variety of offices: one principal — incidentally the only one in the study that reports an outright demonstrative political act of opposition while the party was still entrenched, for which he was rewarded by total isolation on the part of his colleagues — combines church activism with involvement in county government. The other two principals have leading positions in teacher associations, local parties, and county government. All three were involved in the ousting of the communist officials in the county, and one of them was a member of the review board that examined politically incriminated personnel. The small number of counties and principals in this study make it difficult to say if this is a more widespread pattern in other counties as well. Evidence from principals' meetings does suggest, however, that the pattern is more widespread under conditions of 'a weak local democratic personnel base', as a ranking Thüringen state official put it.

According to data from the eight schools, schools that have this politically active type of principal as their leaders are more innovative than others. They develop internal reform activities that are absent at other sites, such as faculty meetings and study groups on pedagogical issues and self-exploration or conspicuous school-wide project weeks.

Summary

Are schools in Eastern Germany democratizing? We tried to find the answer to this question by searching for issues that matter most to educators who have experienced the recent system change in their daily practice at school. We found that the new political democratic order is not a consuming issue for educators, with the exception of a small group of functionaries. We do not know what would have happened if the grassroots reform movement of the years 1989/90 had lasted. Participatory action of the now disillusioned teachers may have flourished. In the subsequent phase of employing the Western model, the teachers' political role clearly became one of passive policy recipients. Teachers try to function as best they can within the institutional shell that the new state authorities provide, hence they are in transition (Zapf, 1992). Their prevalent attitude is obedience rather than allegiance towards the new democratically legitimated authorities. Regardless of some skepticism, Western Germany is the model that educators are oriented towards, and the only alternative to the GDR that is in sight. This model is more convincing economically than culturally and politically. Democratization of schools is not a political movement of conscious educators. Rather, most teachers in the study, with the exception of a few functionaries, define and interpret their role in distinctly a-political terms. Their educational goal is to make students succeed in the new market economy, rather than to make them into successful citizens; they see their teaching as a technical or humanistic process.

Democratization of school site relationships, then, is a product of institutional restructuring and broad-based cultural change in the larger society that sweeps into schools and changes the interaction between teachers and clients. As such, it is a change from 'above' and 'below'. Teachers' authority over parents and students has been shaken. But parents' and students' assertiveness is as much a product of expanded legal rights as it reflects the breaking-up of traditional relationships between generations in the former GDR. As a legacy of past authoritarian experience and present lack of active appropriation of democratic substance, this process takes place with little conscious reflection, much pain, and intolerance on all sides. Hierarchies are crumbling in schools, but both process and outcome are ambivalent with regard to democratization (cf. Weiler, 1993). Most educators are involuntary or reluctant participants in this process.

The organizational structures that fostered socialist paternalism in schools are dismantled. Individualism is boosted. The new school 'business' presumably distributes life chances based solely on meritocratic assumptions rather than on political dependability as well, but may allow for more inequality and segregation. Here again, democratization is ambivalent.

A great challenge for teachers, caused by the new legal framework, new teaching technology, and their past political role, is the reassertion of their professional competence. Various strategies are employed. New knowledge in subject matter, instructional methods, and laws is acquired. Subject matter is reinterpreted in terms of technical expertise and the scientific character of one's academic discipline. The 'West' serves as a performance standard. Comparison with the West is an attractive way of enhancing one's professional standing, but it is repulsive at the same time for its imposing qualities. The new openness and ambiguity forces some hesitant teachers into making new decisions and enthralls others willing to express their new pedagogical freedom.

The current transition period is characterized by teachers' strong subject orientation due to problems of both competence and legitimacy, and as a result of experiencing powerlessness in larger matters both under the previous and the current political system. Hence, policies that tap into teachers' enthusiasm about curriculum and instruction will find more active participation. Likewise, democratization policies that use technical arguments (i.e., appealing to rationally good professional practice) are likely to succeed over the ones that use political arguments.

If one frames, with Guttmann, democratization of school site relations as (re)distribution of authority among the primary actors, teachers, students, parents and the authorities, then teachers are confronted with a loss of authority in some areas and a gain in others. The balance between loss and gain will determine teachers' willingness to actively embrace the process. In the case of Eastern Germany, authorities seem to give full legal–normative support to the democratization of relations at school sites, but retain tight control over the restructuring of the formal organization of schools, stifling teacher participation. By empowering parents and students and by stipulating pluralist sources of knowledge, the authorities sap teachers' traditional moral authority (i.e., their legitimate claim to impose on clients what is right or wrong, good or bad for them). At the same time, the state withdraws from the classroom leaving it up to teachers' professional authority to make decisions based on technical expertise about suitable curriculum delivery. This gain of professional authority, however, is undermined by many teachers' lack of competence in filling out the new space of autonomy. Thus democratization is seen by many teachers more as a threat rather than a boon.

'In the GDR, there was always an answer.' — 'In the GDR, everything was predetermined and foreseeable.' — 'We had one solution to one problem.' The GDR accomplished this sense of security with relatively static, uniform and hierarchical institutions. In this regard, schools in Eastern Germany have now become more like modern democratic institutions. Mobility, individuality, openness and voice of constituencies have increased, but so have uncertainty and strife. The democratization of schools in Eastern Germany remains an ambivalent project.

Chapter 5

The New Structure of Secondary Schools: Macro Politics and Micro Adaptations

For the 1991/92 school term, Land governments in Eastern Germany passed school acts that aligned the Eastern secondary school system to the three-tier structure of West Germany[1]. In implementing the new laws, state governments instructed local agencies to dissolve all polytechnical and extended secondary schools (Polytechnische Oberschule [POS] and Erweiterte Oberschule [EOS]) and reopen them six weeks later as separate elementary and tracked secondary schools. Thousands of teachers, students, desks and textbooks had to be moved and reassembled to compose the new school types. For example, in the state of Brandenburg, 911 polytechnical schools with 322,000 students, and forty-four extended secondary schools (EOS) with 5500 students terminated their existence. Throughout the state, about 22,000 teachers were reassigned to new school types, often to new school sites (Ministerium für Bildung, Jugend und Sport, 1992b, p. 3). In the state of Thüringen, roughly 350,000 students and 30,000 teachers were reassigned to 769 elementary schools, 457 lower-track Regelschulen, 107 college-preparatory Gymnasien, and 122 special schools (often for the learning disabled) (Thüringer Landesamt für Statistik, 1992, p. 4). This reorganization was implemented with remarkable smoothness and was met with great acquiescence on the part of the educators affected (see previous chapter).

The enormous institutional transformation reflected in these numbers involves primarily the creation of new school types that are distinguished by the way they arrange curriculum differentiation and tracking in secondary schools. We will look at this process from two angles: the policy level (i.e., state and local governments), where the new institutional designs are developed, and the school site level (i.e., teachers and principals), where beliefs and practices are adapted to these new institutional forms. We will examine the transformation of the educational system again in two Eastern German states, then center-left governed state of Brandenburg and then center-right governed state of Thüringen[2]. Starting from the same baseline — the highly centralized school system of the GDR —, these two states tried to take a distinctly different approach to the constitution of new school types. Leaving the managerial aspect of the change process aside, we will concentrate in this chapter on pedagogical considerations. This focus involves substantive issues of educational practice and centers on educators as the main implementers of educational reform (see also Mintrop and Weiler, 1994).

Educational researchers in the US have often pointed to the problematic connection between macro and micro levels in the educational system which makes reform implementation difficult (Cuban, 1990). Various theories have attributed this to contradictory policies, especially around issues of equity and selectivity (Carnoy and Levin, 1985; Weiler, 1989), loose coupling (Weick, 1976 and 1982), conflicting constituencies (Wirt and Kirst, 1989), and immutable behavior regularities (Sarason, 1982). Our analysis will be guided by these theories.

In the first part of our analysis, we will briefly deal with government agencies, institutional designs promulgated by the two state governments, and instruments of policy enforcement. The new institutional designs affect educators' traditional views and practices to the degree that they are instituted by 'strong' policies. According to Schwille *et al.* (1988), policy strength depends on the prescriptiveness, consistency, and authority of policy instruments (i.e., laws, curriculum guidelines, testing, student placement, scheduling, textbooks, teacher qualification and staff development). Strong policies compound the effect on crucial teacher decision making domains: time allocation, coverage of topics, student groupings, and standards of achievement (see also Elmore and Sykes, 1992). Schwille's model, generic for curriculum reform, is useful for the case of tracking policies and practices that are at the heart of the system change explored here. The pedagogical domains, specified in the model, have been identified as crucial in many studies of tracking (Oakes, 1985; Page and Valli, 1990; Oakes, Gamoran and Page, 1992). But given the scale of the reform — the institutionalization of whole school type organizations —, the model needs to be expanded. The new school types are bestowed with new institutionalized track charters (Meyer, 1977; Oswald *et al*, 1988) and new organizational opportunity structures (Sorensen, 1970). Those rest on some key elements specific to the school type: student classifications based on sociocultural and ability typifications (Keddie, 1971; Rist, 1977), professional statuses (Finley, 1984; Talbert, 1990; Little, 1993; Philipp and Witjes, 1982; Habel *et al*, 1992), and societal and community expectations (Metz, 1990; Hemmings and Metz, 1990; Oakes, 1985).

While Eastern German governments, as we will see in the first part, are engaged at this point in erecting the institutional shell of the new school types, the second part of the chapter investigates how this shell is filled with life by Eastern German educators. The latter entails an adaptation of teachers' beliefs and practices, steeped in the assumptions and routines of the GDR schools, to the new institutional elements. We will contrast teachers in the 'conservative' state with those in the 'progressive' state, teachers in upper-track schools with those in lower-track schools. We will also see how educators understand the new school type in which they are now working. Four types of schools are examined: the Brandenburg Gymnasium and Gesamtschule (comprehensive school), and the Thüringen Gymnasium and Regelschule (regular school). Our focus is on those aspects of the new schools that relate to the issue of tracking. We will present findings on educators' beliefs about goals, standards, sorting and teaching strategies in these schools. Our findings are based on the study of documents and on about 100 face-to-face interviews with administrators and teachers working at all levels of the system. We concentrated on eight school sites, four Gymnasien (two each in Brandenburg and Thüringen), two Regelschulen in Thüringen, and two Gesamtschulen in Brandenburg.

Setting Up the Institutional Shell

Government Agencies

Two levels of government play a prominent role in the educational reform in the two states: state ministries and local governments (i.e., counties and municipalities). Education falls under the jurisdiction of states in the Federal Republic of Germany although some basic features of the educational system are regulated by federal law and agreements among all federal states (for example, the three-tier structure of school diplomas).

State (Land) and counties (Kreise), or municipalities (Gemeinden) in some cases, are to share in the administration and financing of schools. By law, the state ministry of education regulates and oversees schools in all matters of teaching, learning, and governance according to the will of the state parliament (Landtag). State laws regulate the formal structure of the new school types by certifying teachers, determining instructional and testing schedules, defining student classifications and school career paths, setting admission, promotion and dismissal standards, specifying grouping procedures — to name the most important elements that constitute the blueprint for these school types. The state provides the budget for teaching personnel, sometimes textbooks and governance. State school administrations (Staatliche Schulämter) represent the Ministry of Education in each county. Their directors or superintendents are appointed and supervised by the state. The superintendents hold an administrative position, not a political office.

Counties (and sometimes municipalities), governed by an elected board

(Kreistag), provide the budget for buildings, equipment, and technical support staff. They draw up the local 'school development plan' which determines supply and location of local schools and school type offerings and in turn affects parents' and students' decisions to attend a certain school. This plan can be decisive for a school's 'market' position in relationship to competing schools. Thus a school in either of these states deals in its daily affairs with two administrative agencies, both located in the county: the state school administration for the county and the school division of the county administration, the former dealing mainly with the pedagogical side, the latter with the technical side of schools. In the establishment of schools as in other matters of policy, state and county have to find common ground (see Ministerium für Bildung, Jugend und Sport, 1991, paras. 48–61; Thüringer Kultusministerium, 1991a, paras. 13–15, Thüringer Kultusministerium, 1992a, paras. 1–6).

The state school superintendents in the counties hold a key position in the local implementation of state policies. By law, they are firmly incorporated into the hierarchy of state governmental action even though they are to be sensitive to local conditions. But due to the peculiarities of the East German transition period, it appears that local will and county (and municipal) governments are in a relatively strong position to adjust the states' educational policies to their own local preferences.

States, dissolved in 1952 by the then-GDR authorities, came only into being again in the spring of 1990 as a legal prerequisite for unification with the Western Federal Republic, at a time when the erosion of the communist regime had been well on its way. Prior to that time, counties and municipalities (apart from the central GDR government in Berlin) were the focal points of the political change process. While the central GDR government as well as the superordinate entities above the counties (*Bezirke*) are now defunct, replaced by the federal government in Bonn and the new states, the counties remained as functioning administrative units in the transition from the GDR to the unified Federal Republic[3].

With the ouster of communist party officials, leadership positions were occupied by new personnel at all levels of educational governance. But the process of filling these positions was quite different at each level of government. The ministries in both states were created from scratch. They typically began with (a) a minister, in both cases from the East and connected with the Protestant church; (b) individuals from the minister's political party — sometimes activists in the democracy movement or school practitioners —; (c) a group of West German experts; and (d) a number of technical support staff from former GDR agencies. In Thüringen, more and more ministry positions have been filled by Eastern school practitioners; the new minister himself was a former math teacher. But Western influence remains strong. In Brandenburg, the presence of a strong Western contingent from the West Berlin Green Party ('Die Grünen') was perceptible. In both states the powerful position of the Under-secretary to the Minister of Education was filled by a Westerner; in Brandenburg he came from 'progressive' West Berlin, in Thüringen from 'conservative' Bavaria. Furthermore, the crucial legal departments are staffed by Western personnel.

It was the foremost task of each new ministry to formulate laws and regulations, to create new administrative channels and to forge new links to local authorities. Communication lines were tenuous initially and throughput questionable. However, with the ensuing unification of the country that put structural alignment on the agenda, local reliance on legal and administrative expertise has compensated for the ministries' weak organizational capacity and the political strength of local positions. It is the state ministry that provides essential Western expertise, both legally and administratively.

Counties and municipalities are not only established political structures in the lives of Eastern citizens, but they are also, as far as education is concerned, a legitimate expression of authentic Eastern transformation. In the counties studied in more depth, the leading state superintendents had been active during the democratic upheaval, had participated in local Round Tables, were involved in the actual ouster of the communist party (SED) personnel, or were known as authors of memoranda or manifestoes on local educational change. They were mostly brought to their positions by local political forces — the process being desribed as 'very tumultuous' — and rubberstamped by the ministries. Leaders such as these are educational policy makers in their own right, even though they are officials bound by state regulation. State ministries can impose their will by instructing the state superintendent for the county, but local governments are not mere executioners of state orders.

The Design of Secondary Schools

Thüringen

The Thüringen state government, run then by a center-right party coalition, originally wanted to adopt the traditional three-tier system that is in place in the conservative Western states. But the low level of acceptance of the 'Hauptschule' on the part of parents, the resistance against it on the part of parent and teacher associations as well as the interest of rural areas to keep their local schools viable led to the adoption of a two-tier system. It consists of a college preparatory 'Gymnasium' and a vocational regular school ('Regelschule') that combines two internal tracks under one roof: the lower 'Hauptschule' and the middle 'Realschule'.

The Thüringen school laws (Thüringer Kultusministerium, 1991) stipulate that students are to be admitted to the school types and tracks solely on the basis of grades and academic promise. The three tracks offer a different curriculum with a supposedly different profile that emphasizes academic, technical-clerical, or manual skills and abilities. Each grants only one leaving certificate based on passing a track-specific, state administered central exam. Lower-track and middle-track exams cannot be retaken. Students cannot fulfil the requirements for taking a lower-track exam in a higher track. Failing students will either have to switch into lower tracks or schools and retake classes in profile subjects or leave without a certificate. (Outside the main secondary schools, there are other options to obtain the certificates through trade school and Extended Education schemes.)

In this kind of system, early selection of the right track is crucial for students. At the end of the fourth grade, elementary schools recommend students either for a Gymnasium or a Regelschule career. Roughly a 2.0 grade point average and/or an adequate achievement orientation are required. Students who want to enter a Gymnasium without an elementary school recommendation have to take a special entrance exam. Hence, parental will is constrained by the professional judgment of schools. Trying-out of a track is discouraged; the boundaries between tracks are supposed to be fairly rigid.

The goals of the two main secondary school types in Thüringen are relatively clearly defined relative to each other, in such a way that their special tasks are to be mutually exclusive. The model Gymnasium educates the academically oriented and university-bound students from grade 5 to grade 12, up to grade 9 in core groups, afterwards in courses. According to the brochure (Thüringer Kultusministerium, 1992a) that was distributed by the state to all parents, the Gymnasium emphasizes 'abstract-theoretical problems' that are 'indispensable for studies at the university' and that create 'as well pre-conditions for a professional education outside the university'.

The model Regelschule is the 'heart' (Thüringer Kultusministerium, 1992a) of the system. It educates all others — 'about 65 per cent of Thüringen students' — up to grade 10 after which they enter the job market as apprentices 'as a rule', (except for those students who attend a special school for learning disabled). After sixth grade, these 'others' are again sub-divided into two groups: students of Hauptschule and students of Realschule, following the West German divisions. The law grants school sites two options (i) the integrative model; and (ii) the additive model: in the integrative model, students are only tracked in certain subjects — they need roughly a 3.0 in the subject for the Realschule (middle) course —; in the additive model, students remain in tracked core groups across all subjects they need an overall 3.0 grade point average and academic promise to enter a middle level class. Parent input is desired, but the school makes the final sorting decisions.

Students are classified as Gymnasium, Realschule and Hauptschule students. School types and tracks are associated not only with students' ability to achieve, but also with a certain type of learning aptitude: from more practical, to technical, to theoretical faculties.

Brandenburg

The state of Brandenburg was until 1994 governed by a center-left party coalition. Here, educational policy at the ministerial level is in the hands of educational 'progressives' who, although biased towards the preservation of a common secondary school experience through the massive creation of comprehensive schools (*Gesamtschulen*), conceded to local pressure and to the Liberal Party the resurrection of the *Gymnasium* and then subsequently of the middle-level *Realschule*.

However, according to the school acts (Ministerium für Bildung, Jugend und Sport, 1991), admission to all school types is based on parental choice, not merit. Once admitted, the school has the obligation to educate all students regardless of ability. Removal can only occur with the consent of parents. The same curriculum is to be taught across all school types; in fact the curricula do not even recognize school types; they are designed for grade levels only.

All leaving certificates are granted in all school types based on successful completion of a particular grade level. No formal exams exist for the lower and middle levels, the college admission exam *Abitur* is school-based, albeit supervised by the Ministry. Though students receive a recommendation from their elementary school after the sixth grade, it does not bind parental decision. The school's professional judgment is superseded by parental will. However, early specializations in certain courses (for example, foreign languages) can increase one's school career chances. Classification of students through the Hauptschule/Realschule/Gymnasium labels is avoided in Brandenburg though school type recommendations are given after the sixth grade. The system allows students to aim for a higher track and more easily scale down upon failure, even though a change of schools will still be necessary from a college-bound track into a lower one. Boundaries between tracks are supposed to be more fluid.

Brandenburg thus ended up with three main secondary school types that are more diffuse in their goals (i.e., their tasks are not mutually exclusive, but rather parallel). The Gymnasium — according to the brochure handed out to all parents in the state —

> admits students beginning with grade 7 and dispenses a comprehensive general education in all subjects. The Gymnasium assumes, in

terms of achievement, a more homogeneous student body. This is why it does without forms of differentiation from grades 7 to 10. (Ministerium für Bildung, Jugend und Sport, 1992a, p. 10)

Instruction takes place in supposedly homogeneous core groups, rather than ability-level courses. No information on the final school career goal (such as college preparation) is provided for parents.

The Realschule 'is as a secondary school limited to the lower division (grades 7 through 10). It prepares primarily for a vocational education' (Ministerium für Bildung, Jugend und Sport, 1992a). Successful completion of a Realschule leads to a middle-track leaving certificate. Instruction takes place in core groups.

The Gesamtschule (comprehensive school) 'is a secondary general school for all students' (*ibid*). It offers instruction in core groups and ability-level courses in certain subjects leaving it up to the student to choose from among all school career tracks. 'As a rule the Gesamtschule consists of a lower division (grades 7 through 10) and an upper division *gymnasiale Oberstufe* (grades 11 through 13)' (Ministerium für Bildung, Jugend und Sport, 1991, paragraph 7.2). The model Gesamtschule is the common secondary school for all. Lower, middle, and upper track students are to learn together in the same school and in at least a portion of their classes. Contrary to many of their Western likenesses that offer courses on at least three track levels, emulating the parallel three-tier structure of the other school types, Brandenburg comprehensive schools offer only courses on two track levels, 'basic' and 'extended' (equivalent to Hauptschule and Realschule), into which students are sorted on the basis of grades and academic promise. Three tracks were not feasible due to the small size of the old POS-building stock.

By design, Brandenburg's school types do not operate according to discrete tasks, school career goals, or achievement levels. As a result of this parallelism, parents can choose relatively freely based on their assessment of their child's potential. On the other hand, the school types are bound to either compete with each other for desirable students or to leave undesirables in the hands of others. Gesamtschule and Realschule, as well as Realschule and Gymnasium, compete for middle-track students. Gymnasium and Gesamtschule compete for middle-track and upper-track students.

Both the concept of the Gymnasium and of the Gesamtschule have an inherent design flaw in Brandenburg. On the one hand, the model Gymnasium assumes track homogeneity in the organization of instruction, but the state does not stipulate clear provisions regarding student admission or career goals that would avoid heterogeneity. On the other hand, the model Gesamtschule assumes heterogeneity stipulating open admission and multiple school career opportunities, but the state fosters homogeneity through the organization of instruction (i) by not guaranteeing an upper division (i.e., college-prep instruction beyond tenth grade) in the comprehensive schools; (ii) by making this school type the only one that has a designated lower track, attracting in large numbers students so classified; and (iii) by offering only two tracks in a system with three career options, in effect undermining the college-prep potential of the Gesamtschule. We will see later how practitioners in the schools deal with these ambiguities.

Summary

Both states designed policies for a new secondary school system that are a compromise between the established three-tier system of the Western states, the ideological preferences of the educational camp in power, technical-material constraints due to the legacy of the ex-GDR system, and the power of local political will. The result in Thüringen is a system design of relative inherent clarity: fusing ideas of social hierarchy and meritocracy, it creates two discrete school types with three fairly rigid tracks that correspond to three certified exit options. The result in Brandenburg is a system design of relative inherent ambiguity: fusing ideas of equity and meritocracy, it creates three parallel and competing school types with three fairly loose tracks that do not necessarily correspond with certified exit options. The system design sets up tracks and subverts them at the same time.

Policy Strength

How do states manage the implementation of their school type designs? State ministries in both states are supposed to regulate and oversee all matters of teaching and learning, but the ministries' capacity for handling this task is limited. This is recognized by a number of officials from both states who were interviewed for this study:

> The substantive work of schools is not directed by the Ministry of Education . . . Schools rely on grassroots support. (an official in Thüringen)

> All we are capable of doing is providing the basic structure. (an official in Brandenburg)

Our study has identified four major reasons for these limitations on state action:

(i) support for democratic governance;
(ii) lack of vision;
(iii) limited enforcement;
(iv) parental behavior.

Support for democratic governance

The ministries consider themselves agencies of the new democratic state. Statements of ministry officials as well as official documents show the states' determination not to unduly impede teachers' creativity and freedom in the classroom. Both states want clearly to mark a contrast between them and the tight hierarchical control of the undemocratic GDR.

Thus, state curricular frameworks are relatively open in suggesting teaching content and leave the selection of material, sequence, and emphasis up to teachers[4]. Schools can select from a long list of state approved textbooks, though textbooks are usually specific to the school type. Staff development takes place in relatively independent institutions that offer a whole range of opinions and pedagogical approaches[5]. The arrangement of visits to West German schools is left to professional and local networks although destinations seem to correspond with official state links between the Eastern and Western states.

Lack of vision

The ministries do not make use of informational material to communicate to administrators and practitioners their vision of the new school types. Interviews with newly-recruited Eastern state officials suggest that they themselves have barely moved beyond the stage of comprehending the legal framework, and still lack vision of the new school organizations. On the other hand, Ministry officials from the West, many of them seconded to the East as legal experts, have a grasp of their Western system, but seem to have difficulties at times to understand the mentality of Eastern educators. These problems are symptomatic of a situation in which the system of educational administration constitutes itself at the same time as it reforms the whole educational system.

Limited enforcement

The ministries in either state exert little real influence over the selection and supervision of school personnel. Strong local superintendents, often confirmed in their positions post facto whether they were in agreement with state policies or not, make joint decisions with local governments on the local supply of school types and make most personnel selections for principalships and teaching positions at the new schools. A Brandenburg official comments:

> They don't do what we tell them to do. But can you instruct a superintendent when next day a bunch of people from the county is banging at the door of the minister? It's happened many times.

In Brandenburg, conflicts between local and state governments about the Gymnasium are exacerbated because of divisions along party lines. Within the center-left coalition that governed the state, education was the portfolio of a small radical-democratic party, successor of the East German democracy movement, that is not well represented at the level of local politics. The Ministry, then, found it hard at times to find acceptance for some of its concepts among local politicians.

But even in Thüringen where conflicts do not seem to flare as much, officials express concern about the enforcement of state policies:

> Our influence on the reorganization plan of the county is not all that great. Many school superintendents must learn that they are our people, not the county president's (Landrat). . . . We are in the process of reeducating principals and school superintendents in this direction.

State officials report that superintendents are called in to the Ministry from time to time, but no regular local inspection is conducted. Contact of the Ministry with local governments and schools seems to be restricted to crisis intervention and frequent counseling in legal-administrative matters.

While principals at the schools we studied stay in close touch with their superintendents on legal and organizational matters, they shun supervising instruction and evaluating teachers at their sites. As long as teachers outwardly comply with general legal guidelines they are very much left alone in pedagogical matters.

For the most part, ministries in either state rely for the implementation of their school type concepts on mandating a specific formal organizational structure, counting on the voluntary compliance of subordinate levels with those mandates.

Parental behavior

When the new schools opened, Gymnasien experienced an onslaught of parents intent on enrolling their children regardless of teacher recommendations. The 'open admission' feature of the Brandenburg Gymnasium design accommodates those parents' wishes. However, grouping structures assume achievement homogeneity, and are thus not easily adjusted to the resulting heterogeneity of the student body. Furthermore, a tendency of parents to shun the local Gesamtschulen for middle-track Realschulen, where available, undermined the integrative potential of the comprehensive schools.

In Thüringen, the stipulated clear distinction between Gymnasium and Regelschule was lost when the state was reportedly not able to enforce its strict admission criteria against the pressure of parents and court rulings that reinforced parents' rights. The state, however, is intent on rolling back the initial openness of Gymnasium admissions. Nevertheless, Thüringen Gymnasien are even more beset by the conflict between a potential achievement heterogeneity of their student body and an organizational design that is based more on academic exclusivity.

Some Local Examples

Thüringen

In one Thüringen county, superintendents and some principals of the existing former GDR schools (POS) drew up the school development plan. Initially, the county designed two plans: one for a three-tier system and another for a two-tier system. They were ready to comply with whatever the school law-in-the-making would regulate. Local politicians and administrators coming from various parties (CDU, SPD, FDP) — the county is governed by a grand coalition comprising all of them — were in basic agreement with state policies.

The two-school-type version of the law, when it finally passed, was a clear guideline for the new structure of the system. Projections for attendance at the college-prep Gymnasium were taken from the experience of a conservative Western state, Bavaria. Conflicts arose within the county over the maintenance of state minimum-size standards for schools. Those standards made Regelschulen in small villages untenable, a conflict that haunted many counties and forced the state to grant many exceptions to the organizational design of rural schools.

The local 'school development plan' had to be reworked when it became clear that the state could not enforce that portion of the law that regulates admission to the Gymnasium. As a result, parental will, and not academic merit as the law had stipulated, decided over school attendance in this first wave of restructuring. The percentage of children slated for the

Gymnasium soared to over 50 per cent in this locality, a percentage that appears to be the norm for non-rural areas in both states regardless of state design (Thüringer Landesamt für Statistik, 1992; Ministerium für Bildung, Jugend und Sport, 1992b).

Achievement criteria for tracking students into the two school types have not been enforced so far. This has the effect that (i) the Gymnasium does not achieve the homogeneity that its concept requires; and (ii) the Regelschule competes with the Gymnasium for the student population in the middle range of achievement. With achievement-based admissions criteria in limbo and with large Gymnasium organizations and their own dynamic of self-preservation established, the outcome of this competition is not clear. The new system in Thüringen has at least initially forfeited its intended clarity. The hierarchy of tracks has in reality become more diffuse than the original design suggested.

Brandenburg

The Brandenburg State Ministry faced local opposition against its favoritism of comprehensive schools right from the beginning. Many county authorities wanted a strong college-prep Gymnasium, sometimes as a showcase for their county seats. They received support from vocal parent groups.

In one county where the leading superintendents reportedly disagreed with the equity orientation of the Ministry and advocated strong upper and middle tracks, the local comprehensive school has to deal with a burgeoning Gymnasium and a Realschule right next door. In this county, the Gesamtschulen are without a college-prep upper division. In another county, comprehensive schools had college-prep upper division grade levels, but the local Gymnasium principal was given a freehand by the county in assembling a faculty of particularly committed teachers from the applicant pool. Parents had organized demonstrations to the state capital in favor of a Gymnasium. In yet another county, the Gesamtschule in one municipality successfully waged a fight for a college-prep upper division against the conservative county government. An alliance consisting of the municipality, a vocal parent group, the school, and the moral support of the Ministry prevailed over the county, which for its part proceeded to spend scarce resources on refurbishing the Gymnasium building located at the county seat.

These examples illustrate the conflicts that arose in Brandenburg about the shape of the new school system and the nature of the new ways of tracking. The somewhat contradictory nature of the school laws leaves ample room for divergent interpretation and contestation of the law at the local level.

Summary

State ministries determine the formal structure of the new school types by making many of its key elements legally binding. Being in the process of formation themselves, the ministries rely on voluntary local consent and law-abidance rather than control. Local variation within the boundaries of the law seems frequent. At this point, state intervention in the substantive core of teaching and learning is limited and indirect, and is only loosely linked to technical support schemes. In both states, the new schools evolving from a combination of organizational blueprints and parental behavior are inherently ambiguous, in the 'progressive' state more by design, in the 'conservative' state more by default.

So far in our analysis, the establishment of the new school types has been limited to treating them as organizational shells: a building and material resources were secured; principal, teachers, and students were assigned; curricula, textbooks, schedules, and groupings were determined; a categorical designation was conferred on it; and finally the shell was placed in the vicinity of other differently named shells. In the next section, we will show how educators interpret these shells and fill them with life.

Making the Shell Work

The Acceptance of Tracking

Most educators, administrators and politicians stress student achievement as the overarching goal of schools. The more extensive interviews show a clear connection between this orientation and the belief that the GDR as a societal order failed because it was not economically competitive with the West. Because the competitive market society lets talents rise to the top, it proved to be stronger in the end. We found this economic argument to be common among former friends and foes of the GDR. A Gymnasium teacher who may stand for many states the argument like this:

> When I travelled to the West for the first time I was ashamed. I was in a country where everybody spoke German, and everything was so well kept and spruced up. What have we done all these years? I don't care about exploitation of man by man as long as everybody is doing better. — Social welfare and security comes only with economic productivity.

The same argument claims that the former polytechnical schools (POS) reflected this major shortcoming of the socialist system. Schools promoted social levelling (*Gleichmacherei*) by neglecting top students and by artificially raising the bottom. There was only one tightly prescribed curriculum for all students up to the tenth grade. Ability grouping within heterogeneous classrooms was not widely practiced. Many educators, then, look back with disappointment at their experience of heterogeneous classrooms and find teaching homogeneous groups easier and more rewarding, like this lower-track teacher in Thüringen:

> The top was always bored and didn't have to do much, the bottom always hobbled along, never catching up. Now everybody gets a chance to succeed.

Teachers were held accountable by principals and the authorities for student failure. As a teacher put it: 'An F for the student was an F for the teacher.' Teachers were to go to great lengths to make a student pass the tenth grade. As a consequence, many failing students were coddled and passed on regardless. While teachers scorn the GDR for the practice of blaming the teacher and suppressing the reality of failure, the ethic of caring for the weak runs deep and is still vaunted by many. The following comments, recorded in all school types, reveal the difficult transition of Eastern German educators in their dealing with student failure:

- We have to fight against sympathy to judge students objectively.
- We really should become harder.
- We had to fight for each student. Now there is the tendency: okay, if he doesn't want to . . .
- We GDR teachers are used to be guided by the weaker ones. Our orientation is helping. I can't let them fall through the cracks.
- We can finally grade as one is supposed to. One isn't called in anymore when a student fails the exam.

Although teachers are still struggling with the traditional values of inclusion and social integration, tracking based on academic merit or differentiating students into homogenous groups according to learning ability is — at least as an idea — almost undisputed. This accounts for the broad acceptance — in general principle, that is — of the stratified educational system of West Germany.

At the same time, this acceptance of the idea of tracking based on merit is not accompanied by actual selection practices. Failure and retention rates in the schools we visited were very low — except perhaps for students in the lowest track.

The static nature of the socialist economy made it possible that the educational system was relatively well articulated with the economy. It was the state's task to make sure that at the end of the students' school career everyone had an apprenticeship or job position commensurate with their perceived ability and the needs of the economy, and teachers had to assist in this task. The close link between school and economy has now been severed, and a new sorting mechanism, a competitive labor market, has been thrust upon East German students and their teachers.

Educators in our study take different approaches to this new situation. One cluster of teachers 'doesn't know what to make of it all'. One very small cluster advocates an educational system with great flexibility that leaves students' options open; and a sizable cluster — with principals overrepresented and more outspoken here — sees tracks as a good way to channel students into their station.

Discussions with educators of this third cluster harken back to the idea that tracks relate to types of human aptitude and that the successful completion of a track or school type will or should translate into an entry position on the hierarchical job ladder that corresponds with student ability types: abstract-theoretical versus concrete-practical. Tracks reflect the economy: 'The job landscape is subdivided, hence we need a subdivided school system', one Thüringen principal puts it. In the view of many upper-track and lower-track educators, the sphere of academia and higher education seems more elevated and distant from the great majority of positions so that this sphere warrants a separate secondary school type, the Gymnasium, while the rest can be educated together in another school type. This view mirrors the old division between the polytechnical school as the school for all, and the extended secondary school as the school for the select few. (This view may also reflect the 'official' class structure of the GDR that divided the society into 'working class' and 'peasantry' allied with the 'socialist intelligentsia' of which teachers were members (Meier, 1990; Berger, 1991).)

But the idea of congruence between job and school hierarchies runs into trouble. Neither parents and students at one end, nor employers at the other end of the schooling process behave according to this model. Educational and economic systems do not seem to fit. Teachers deplore that parents and students find the lowest-track education unacceptable and flock to the college-prep tracks and school types although they have no aspirations for a university education. Employers shun lower-track graduates although their qualification actually fits the job that is offered. Many argue like this small town teacher:

> The institutions that succeed schools must take advantage of the differentiation of the educational system. It is bad when our local savings and loan hires only graduates that hold a university admission

degree (Abiturienten). The business community here has difficulties understanding the new educational system.

In the face of troubling discontinuities between economy and education, these teachers call for business and parents to behave according to the unambiguous sorting mechanisms of the hierarchical school system. As a last resort, the state is brought back to create order. In an exchange between a critic and a proponent of tracking, the critic pointed out that lowest-track graduates are faced with a 'social out'. The proponent retorted, 'The state would never waste all these talents.'

Although the new tracked system — despite its problematic features — is widely accepted among educators to whom we spoke, teachers working in upper-track schools experience it differently from teachers in lower-track schools. To this contrast we turn next.

Gymnasium

The Gymnasium is many things to many educators. For some educators, notably the principals that were interviewed, 'Gymnasium' is a powerful label that symbolizes the academic tradition of the country that was lost under socialism, and stands for the new era because it, more than any other school type, breaks away from the social levelling of the GDR schools. Many educators want the Gymnasium housed in the old 'venerable' school buildings of the county where it can, indeed, be found in many instances. Others, more skeptical of the ways of the West and loath of 'false status thinking', stress the technical aspect of the Gymnasium as an educational setting for college-bound students. Both positions, represented in about equal strength in both states, voice more affinity with the academic Gymnasium concept of Thüringen than with the open Gymnasium concept of Brandenburg.

Student body composition

In both Thüringen and Brandenburg, the view is widely shared among Gynasium teachers that 'this is not a real Gymnasium'. The most frequently voiced complaint is that everybody can come to the Gymnasium regardless of academic merit. Students that have marginal ability, look forward to entering an apprenticeship rather than a university, or are still at the school because they have not yet found employment are considered misplaced. The task of the Gymnasium, after all, is seen as preparing students for successful study at a university. It is unimaginable for most educators in the study — teachers, principals, but also superintendents — that 50 per cent of the secondary school population, this being the percentage of Gymnasium students in many localities, could be 'college-prep material'. One Brandenburg superintendent explains it this way:

> Seven per cent as in the GDR was too low (the GDR figure for the attendance of Extended Secondary Schools — EOS); 15 per cent are really deserving, 10 per cent go along with it; 10 per cent are a concession to public pressure; but 50 per cent (the figure of Gymnasium attendance in his district) is way too high.

With a norm of 35 per cent, or about one-third of the student population allocated to the highest track in the three-tier system, this Brandenburg superintendent is in line with the target figure touted, but not enforced by the Ministry in Thüringen (Thüringer Kultusministerium, 1992b, p. 5).

Teachers and principals in both states attribute the 'false composition' of their student body to parents that send their undeserving children to the Gymnasium despite lack of ability. Teachers often assume 'prestige' as the motivating factor for parents, implying that parents try to obtain social status with false pretenses. In Brandenburg, responsibility is also assigned to the open admission policies of the ministry that seems determined 'to ignore the achievement principle (Leistungsprinzip) in schools when it is now valid in all other areas of society'. The Thüringen Ministry is assumed to be more on the side of the 'real Gymnasium'. Both ministries are scolded by teachers for unclear guidelines and administrative incompetence, but educators express faithful adherence to state mandates in both states. In addition, many Gymnasium teachers think that elementary school teachers are 'too easy', that a strict orientation level in grades 5 and 6 is needed, and that unfortunately the lower-track schools, embattled with behavioral problems, are 'no alternative for parents'.

In both states, then, it is up to the individual school sites to attract the right kind of students by setting standards that they deem appropriate for their Gymnasium. This means that each individual teacher in his/her classroom is called upon to uphold standards that secure the school's reputation in the community. Principals voiced these expectations of teachers, and many Gymnasium teachers were acutely aware of the issue.

Teachers imagine the typical Gymnasium student to have the requisite grades, an abstract-theoretical aptitude, a willingness to learn, and a considerable measure of self-direction. Some teachers feel that grades and learning ability alone do not make a Gymnasium student. They add to this catalogue orderly conduct and believe that discipline problems ought not to exist at a 'real Gymnasium'. Whereas the new legal principles separate norms of conduct from academic performance, the latter being the sole basis of advancement, many teachers in the study want to see a combination of the two in Gymnasium students, as was the case for Extended Secondary School (EOS) students. For many teachers, the reality of their Gymnasium looks very different from their original expectations although the extent of the discrepancy varies by school. Educators complain that students are undisciplined, that the assumption of a favorable disposition toward learning on the part of students was an illusion, and that they encounter wide heterogeneity in their classes.

Many teachers who used to teach in the select Extended Secondary School (EOS) experience teaching these Gymnasium students as a deterioration compared to their former well-behaved and high-performing students. Former POS teachers without college-prep experience — the majority of the faculty at Gymnasien — report that the instructional level for Gymnasium students is not very far from the old polytechnical school. Some in this group even believe that the Gymnasium actually ranks below the POS.

Gauging standards

How do teachers know what level of teaching content is appropriate for a Gymnasium? Some find their orientation in the new Western Gymnasium textbooks. State curricula or in-service training are not mentioned. A larger group asserts that 'all teachers have gone through the EOS as students, so they know what's required'. For former EOS teachers generally, this question does not seem to pose a problem. They were the real college-prep teachers before the 'Wende'. At sites where former POS teachers harmonize with former EOS-teachers, teachers report learning from the EOS experience through their colleagues in their departments. At one site, conflicts initially erupted between ex-EOS and ex-POS staff. While the EOS teachers assumed that the new Gymnasium was theirs to shape, the POS teachers felt treated as second class citizens by colleagues whom they perceived as part of the former 'red' elite. (This type of conflict was mentioned again at principal retreats.) At one site — incidentally the one that was definitely the most active and innovative school among the eight we saw — none of the newly-assigned teachers, including the principal, came from a college-prep EOS. Here an optimistic and defiant mood of 'We are all learning' prevailed.

Another source of orientation for Gymnasium standards is a comparison with Western schools. Some schools, particularly in Brandenburg, have extensive contacts with Western Gymnasien; almost all teachers and all principals in the study have visited Western schools; educators stress frequently that their Gymnasium looks as good in terms of standards as the ones they saw in the West.

Upholding standards

Up to ninth grade in Thüringen or tenth grade in Brandenburg, students in the Gymnasium are taught in core groups that stay together all day and are instructed as one group in almost all their subjects. Despite heterogeneity in their classes — heterogeneity that has decreased by POS standards, but increased by EOS standards — teachers do not report within-class ability grouping, or other deliberate support systems as techniques for curriculum delivery. 'Förderkurse' (special courses for remediation and enrichment) do exist, but do not seem to be widespread. In all classes we observed, one lesson was taught to all students in the class. After all, the Gymnasium is, in the eyes of teachers, already a tracked school, or at least is supposed to be. On the whole, Gymnasium educators stress continuity in their teaching practice over reform; as a result, the delivery of a teacher-centered unitary curriculum is reinforced. There are no traceable differences between the two states in this regard. Former EOS teachers, having taught only grades 11 and 12, report having to adjust to the new age groups of the lower grade levels and speak of downscaling the curriculum. Some former POS teachers report cutting back on practice time, moving along a little faster, dispensing with regular work checks, and insisting on students finding the answer themselves as opposed to simply reproducing it. Responses on subject matter are not consistent. Some teachers say they increased the amount of subject matter covered, others deny this[6].

How do teachers, then, calibrate the level of difficulty for their lessons? On the one hand, many of them want to adhere to high EOS/college-prep standards; on the other hand, they admit the performance level is not adequate for such a curriculum. A range of positions exists in the schools on how to approach this dilemma, with no detectable differences between the two states. Some teachers emphasize the school's track status, some the concerns of students, and others grapple with their old practices, as the following comments from four Gymnasium sites illustrate.

The teachers who aspire to the new track status:

> You can't gauge your lessons for mediocrity like we did in the POS.
> We teachers from the POS always try that everybody understands it. One has to think differently.
> I am always afraid I underchallenge students at the Gymnasium.

The teachers who resist the new status expectations:

> Performance standards are a result of the average. You need to try out what students can do.

It is the meaning of teaching that as many students as possible understand.

We can't punish the students for something that is not their fault. They can't do anything about being in the wrong place.

The teachers who enforce the new track standards:

It's time to start to kick them out.

There's nothing you can do about it. Students are retained twice and then they must leave the school.

We would like to get rid of the weak ones.

We just don't have enough failures.

Students should not be able to compensate an F (in one subject with an A or B in another, as is the law).

We have so many failures because the wrong people come.

I don't want my students to shame me when they get to the university.

The principals as well as the superintendents in both states who were interviewed regretted that despite all the teachers' complaints about a lack of standards, the number of failures at all the Gymnasien is incredibly low. There are no differences between the sites in the two states in this regard. For example, in one Thüringen Gymnasium with over 1000 students only a handful failed the grade. How can this be explained? Referring to the quotes above, the number of teachers resisting the new track status at the sites is relatively small and not very outspoken, while the teachers willing to enforce them are — at least in this study — stronger in number and in leadership positions; it is possible that the ones aspiring to the new status have not made quite the transition they describe.

Discussions with a number of teachers about this point suggest that professional norms against casting out failures dating from the GDR, and particularly prevalent in the old polytechnical schools, are still quite strong. Teachers' meritocratic orientations are challenged, but not necessarily submerged by norms of equity and inclusion. Teachers want the system to take care of the dirty work; strict selection for the college-prep track, no repetition of exams, no compensation for final Fs are popular among a sizable group of teachers. Yet their grading standards in their classes do not seem to match this perspective. An older science teacher seems characteristic in this regard. She is very active in after-school projects with students; she wants to have her old EOS back, and for that she needs to get rid of many of her students. But did that mean that she had to 'decimate'? In the old

The New Structure of Secondary Schools

days, once a student made it into the selective EOS, success was virtually guaranteed.

Other explanations were aired. When the Eastern '1' through '5' grading scale was aligned with the West to include a '6' for complete failure, the statutes that regulate promotion and retention (based on the Western grading scale from '1' to '6') did not match Eastern grading routines and expectations anymore. A teacher describes: 'When a student is in danger of receiving a "4", an alarm goes off in our minds. In the GDR you had to act then.' In addition, students expect the higher GDR grades.

An interesting facet revealed itself only after inquiring in other school types. Generally, bad grades cumulate in the lowest track while the middle and upper (Gymnasium) track have few failures. Rather than grading on track specific or school-type specific criteria, many Eastern German teachers apply their traditional unitary POS-standards. On that basis, Gymnasium students are always bound to be above average. This practice reveals how imperfectly teachers in the East have as yet absorbed the logic underlying the fully institutionalized tracking system of the West, where student categorizations (for example, Gymnasium student) would be considered classes *sui generis*.

Another point was usually hinted at more surreptitiously, but well articulated by an activist for the professional association of Gymnasium teachers:

We want to maintain the standards of the Gymnasium and want to avoid the hemorrhage of the Regelschule (lower-track school type). We have more students than we should have. So on the one hand we want higher standards, but on the other hand I am a union man, and we need to secure jobs. Every teacher resolves this individually. Every school tries to get as many students as possible in order to avoid job reduction.

Student enrolment will dramatically decline in years to come due to a plunge in fertility rates in the East and migration to the West (Klemm *et al*, 1992). Gymnasium teachers are in a bind. They want the status of a Gymnasium, but the enforcement of rigid standards increases the likelihood of losing one's job at the Gymnasium. Particularly former POS teachers are faced with reassignment to a lower-track school.

Status

What does it mean to teachers to be 'Gymnasium teachers'? There are those for whom teaching at this school type is 'something special', or for whom this school type is 'their rightful place to be' because they have 'more to offer' than the average teacher, like EOS experience or a PhD. Then there are those for whom being at this school type is a matter of luck since they can enjoy better working conditions than teachers at other school types. The majority of informants being queried about this point falls into this category. Lastly, there is a group of teachers — conspicuously more women than men, and more former POS than EOS teachers — who are at the Gymnasium for reasons of convenience: mainly being close to home.

With the exception of the first group, a clear sense of elevated professional status among Gymnasium teachers was not in strong evidence. The experience of being 'cut from the same mould' as the other teachers — in the GDR, all teachers had the same preparation and most of them taught at a polytechnical school — as well as the widespread experience of being arbitrarily assigned to their new school militates against the identification with a new status. However, new incoming Gymnasium teachers, trained under the West German model, will have more academic and practical training.

Summary

The meritocratic orientation of many Gymnasium educators in general facilitates the implementation of a stratified educational system. Specifically, teachers in both states model their school after a diffuse pre-socialist tradition, their own college-prep GDR experience, conditions of teaching and learning in the old extended secondary school (EOS), and a rudimentary knowledge of Western schools. The implementation of this diffuse selective model of a college-preparatory school is hampered by the contrast between a heterogeneous student body and an internal organizational structure that reinforces expectations of homogeneity in instruction. Professional norms of inclusion, routines of lesson delivery and grading, and considerations of job security counteract the adoption of selective practices that would be a prerequisite for the aspired status.

In both states, the schools we studied adhere to the notion of an 'academic Gymnasium' in theory and operate an unacknowledged and involuntary 'open Gymnasium' in practice, in Brandenburg due to state guidelines of the Ministry, in Thüringen as a result of unenforced track boundaries. The Thüringen model of an academic Gymnasium finds easier acceptance among educators. But in neither state were the specific designs of the ministry as yet implemented. In Thüringen, the ministry's promulgation of the principle of a selective Gymnasium does not appear to translate into selective practices. In Brandenburg, the open model of a Gymnasium that is implied in the Ministry regulations is rejected or ignored by most educators. Few specific allowances are made that acknowledge heterogeneity as a lasting structural element of this school type. Schools in both states 'muddle through' in the face of a high degree of ambiguity.

Regelschule and Gesamtschule

The Thüringen Regelschule

Concurring with the official design of the state, the Thüringen Regelschule is seen by most educators in the study as an institution for students who aspire to or are capable of apprenticeship positions in the lower or middle range of the economic job ladder. Thüringen Regelschule teachers envision their schools to be the place for all students that are non-college-preparatory. They largely accept the split between the Gymnasium educating the academic top and their school educating all others, as is stipulated in the state system design. Two arguments that speak for this institutional split are mentioned by our informants: (i) schools that educate all three tracks would become too big; 500 students per school seems to be the maximum for most educators we talked to, and with that size three tracks could simply not be accommodated; (ii) the difference between college-prep and non-college-prep is big enough that it warrants two different school types while the difference between the lower-track Hauptschule and the middle-track Realschule does not. They can more easily be housed within the same school type. Both arguments seem again to reflect GDR experience. The preferred school size argument corresponds to POS conditions, and the school type split in Thüringen is similar to the one between POS (common school for all) and EOS (upper division college-prep), as was pointed out earlier. Many informants consider the Regelschule something 'specifically Thüringian', that is, neither a copy of the Western three-tier system (since it combines lower and middle tracks), nor a new version of the old socialist unitary school (since it excludes the college-prep students). It is, in the words of one educator, 'a POS minus the top'.

Like the polytechnical school (POS) used to be, the state of Thüringen has declared the Regelschule the 'heart' of the educational system. But for many teachers and principals at these schools this does not concur with their experience. They feel they should educate the vast majority of the students, and deplore the fact that so many middle-range talents have found admission to the Gymnasium where they do not belong while the Regelschule is left with 'the rest' and all the social problems that result from this distribution. Two solutions for this problem are suggested: a small cluster of educators feels confirmed in its advocacy of some kind of differentiated comprehensive school, but a large majority wants to see strict boundaries enforced between the Gymnasium and the Regelschule that would channel more students into the lower-level Regelschule. Most educators, especially the principals in the study, are aware that their Regelschule will have to make a special effort of establishing a good public 'profile' in order to compete with the Gymnasium. The Ministry is accused of allowing track boundaries to slip. A frequently told joke among Regelschule educators is that the state considers the Regelschule the 'heart' and the Gymnasium the 'face' of the new system. It ends with the punchline: But see for yourself how much attention we usually give to our hearts and how much to our faces.

The Brandenburg Gesamtschule

The Gesamtschule in Brandenburg is beset with problems similar to the ones found in the Regelschule. But these problems are perceived by Gesamtschule educators with more intensity there because reality conflicts even more strongly with the comprehensive claims of the state design. We studied two types of Gesamtschule, one school without a college-prep upper-division that is located in the immediate vicinity of a Realschule and a Gymnasium, and one school with college-prep grade levels 11 through 13 that is the only secondary school in a small rural municipality.

The faculty in the first location is the most cohesive among all eight schools we visited. When the school, a former POS, was redesignated a Gesamtschule, most teachers of the middle grades chose to stay and to create a new school together with a number of new colleagues: a school that was comprehensive, but based on achievement. The former principal, already on duty during the times of the old party regime, retained his post. According to the interviews, the school envisioned to attract students of all abilities by becoming a magnet for foreign languages in the municipality. These ideas, however, did not come to fruition. Educators pointed out that the local school development plan did not grant them a college-prep division, scarce foreign language teachers are concentrated at the local Gymnasium, and the burgeoning local Realschule and Gymnasium siphon off middle-range students. Parents, the educators surmise, consider the Gesamtschule as being too similar to the old socialist unitary school whereas the other schools, representing elevated track status, represent the new market society. The school now sees a danger of developing into a low-level Hauptschule in substance.

Educators in this school expressed great disillusionment about their school type. Many teachers stated that the Gesamtschule is a 'failed model'; they resented the allegedly discriminatory treatment they receive from the local superintendent's office, and they scorned the state ministry as inept and inefficient at coming out in support of their own policy design. On the other hand, those same educators did not question the need for a 'real'

Gymnasium that is truly college-preparatory. They thought they can play a special college-prep role for those students that are initially designated middle-track students, but show greater promise later on in their careers. The middle-track Realschule, however, was considered completely superfluous. The interview with the principal is revealing:

> We hail from doctrinaire times, but even now we have little discretion. Things are prescribed for us, but the teacher colleagues don't fight it. A rigid system has again been superimposed. We didn't want the three tiers because it makes the Gesamtschule into a Hauptschule. The idea of the comprehensive school has perished. Nobody intended that. Frau Birthler (the then Minister of Education) meant well, but . . . Maybe the Sachsen-Thüringen model is better. Here, the Realschule thinks it's something better. It's been an obsolete tradition (alter Zopf) for centuries. Parents tell me, 'We would like to come to your school, Mr. XXX, but you need to have a different label for your school.' . . . So we have all the problem cases of the town. . . . It is easier to get a higher grade at a Gesamtschule because our student-teacher ratio is better due to the courses. . . . We would like to prove ourselves as a Gesamtschule, but it's difficult with this student material.
>
> We had a good reputation when we were POS, but now the reputation of the Gesamtschule in Brandenburg is bad. . . . The Gymnasium is absolutely necessary because gifted children should go to a separate school. Maybe it's possible to live without a Hauptschule, but my daughter is not going to go to a Gesamtschule. She needs to learn how to work as a scientist at a Gymnasium. Without that, no Nobel prize has ever been won.

Educators in the other Gesamtschule that we studied were not as sanguine about the Gymnasium. As the only secondary school at the location and with the nearest Gymnasium ten miles away, this school wants to prove it can be college-prep. But despite the better 'market' conditions for this school, defensiveness prevails. The county government has repeatedly tried to cut the college-prep division of the school and to channel college-prep students into the Gymnasium located at the seat of the county. In addition, the old EOS was located in the county seat, and no teacher with experience in taking students to the *Abitur* has been assigned to the Gesamtschule; thus, this ex-POS-only faculty has a legitimacy problem that is exacerbated by having to accommodate lower-track students as well as upper-track ones. At this school, however, we found teachers who think their own children better placed in a Gesamtschule than in a Gymnasium. Yet, teachers felt insecure whether they would succeed in maintaining a sufficient number of students for their college-prep division or revert to the more standard lower-middle-track version of a Gesamtschule. In both this school and the other Gesamtschule we visited in Brandenburg, reality and policy design were at considerable variance, and further development is uncertain.

Internal tracking

While the Thüringen and Brandenburg lower-level schools vary in the degree of goal ambiguity, they are alike in many respects. All four schools we visited had the overwhelming majority of their students placed in the middle (Realschule) track which is their upper track; only in one Gesamtschule was the balance tilting towards the lower (Hauptschule) tracks. Educators in all these schools stated that their upper tracks had to be protected at all cost. They are seen as a constitutive element of the school profile and as such crucial in wooing parents eager for their child's education to the school, and are a relief from the novel and overwhelming discipline problems that teachers have to cope with in these schools. One strategy of elevating the upper track is isolating 'problem students' in the lowest track.

In Thüringen, Regelschulen can set up tracked core groups or strands that stay together all day long for a whole school year. In one Regelschule that uses the core group model for internal tracking, the seventh grade Hauptschule class that we observed was an all-boys class with an unusually wide age range because of the number of grade repeaters in it. According to the teachers, failure across the board in this class is rampant. We gained the impression that the school had created here a virtual dumping ground that was, according to teachers' comments, unmanageable for regular teaching. The core group model for internal tracking was popular among teachers in this school for various reasons: some pointed to the above mentioned strategy of sheltering the Realschule track; other teachers, reminiscing about the class collectives of the POS, did not like the loosening of social ties that the alternative of a course model would entail; the principal pointed to another issue:

> The additive (core group based) model of tracking is easier to organize. The courses are a scheduling nightmare, and take up a lot more teacher hours. If we have at least fourteen students in the Hauptschule in each grade level, we can go with core groups.

He went on to say that, as far as he is concerned, these lowest-track Hauptschule classes will not receive any special treatment or favors from the school. They would have to achieve and behave like everybody else. He indicated that in the past educators had been too lenient. A few teachers that we interviewed at that school, however, were unhappy with the modus of internal tracking because it cannot accommodate students that are borderline (i.e., good in one subject and bad in another).

In Thüringen, where the internal tracks of the Regelschule correspond by name with the established school types of the West and where a different curriculum is taught in each track, the correct classification of students was of heightened concern. Who ends up as a Hauptschule student in the lower courses or lower core group is decided by teachers on the basis of grades and learning potential. Asked about the permeability of tracks, a principal who rejects the core-group tracking model as socially too severe, nevertheless commented:

> There is not much switching between courses at the school. If there was, we would be bad professionals. It would show that we would not be able to make the right decisions for our students.

In Thüringen Regelschulen, then, the state design of the educational system (i.e., the delimited perspective of the Regelschule as well as the fairly rigid tracking structure) tended to resonate with educators' orientation of channeling students into their rightful tracks rather than fostering their upward mobility.

In Brandenburg, the situation is somewhat different. Any aspirations for a Gesamtschule to attain or retain college-prep status is contingent upon the school's ability to recruit and produce a sufficient number of students ready for a college-prep curriculum. Thus, we found expectations of student mobility more often expressed in the Gesamtschulen than in the Thüringen Regelschulen. But even in the former where students by law are to be tracked for only a portion of the time we encountered the existence of honors core groups in one of the schools (the college-prep one). This semi-legal practice was justified as a concession to the academically inclined and vocal parents on whose political support the school relies.

In both Gesamtschulen, the idea of changing the school system by establishing a separate low-level Hauptschule was popular among educators. The argument goes: since Brandenburg already has an upper-track Gymnasium and a middle-track Realschule, it needs a lower-track Hauptschule; in such a system, the Gesamtschule would occupy a special niche attracting parents that agree with its social philosophy of social integration or whose children are potential 'late bloomers' — a situation similar to some Western states. The creation of a separate Hauptschule was rejected by those few that see its potential for segregating ethnic immigrant minorities from the German majority. Generally speaking, however, despite state designs that promulgate the permeability of tracks and the mobility of students, we found educators

85

in Brandenburg as concerned with establishing status and erecting boundaries as their colleagues in Thüringen.

Gauging and enforcing standards

How do teachers know what constitutes the adequate curriculum for a given track? Here again, we encountered the same elements as were described for the Gymnasium: traditional GDR standards, the new textbooks, and the comparison with Western schools. Textbooks were not mentioned as often, but the GDR school is:

> I know the standards from the last twenty years of teaching in a POS. Those are my standards.

Educators in both Regelschule and Gesamtschule reported again and again about having a hard time 'upholding POS standards' in schools now that they are faced with a concentration of unruly and less willing students. A lower-track teacher reported:

> When they split up our POS we knew we would get the ones that didn't do as well. But we thought they would work harder in the new achievement society (*Leistungsgesellschaft*). The opposite has happened.

In schools where contacts with Western schools have occurred, teachers pointed out that their standards are adequate to, if not higher than, Western standards.

Students who do not measure up to these established standards are relegated to the lower-track classes or courses. This is supposed to happen solely on the basis of academic achievement, but there are indications — such as the conspicuous overrepresentation of boys in the lower track in some schools — that behavioral standards of sorts play a role as well. The seeming facility with which educators in both states have adopted Western categorical labeling of students for their own terminology — as Hauptschule, Realschule, and Gymnasium students — is striking, but contrasts with a more difficult transition of educational practice, as evidenced by grading practices and lesson delivery. While some teachers have developed track-specific criteria, others still apply the unitary standards of the POS.

Two ways of grading exist side-by-side in the same school: some educators reported grades ranging from 'B' through 'D' in the (internal) upper track, and 'C' through 'F' in the (internal) lower track, with an emphasis on failing grades. The rationale most often heard is that the top students have gone to the Gymnasium, therefore 'As' are not possible, and that the lower level students cannot follow the curriculum. This kind of a unitary grading scale across tracks and maybe school types is a heritage of the unitary school. This practice was disputed by a smaller group of teachers who felt that an 'A' would be justified in the lowest track since the students themselves are a completely different category.

Generally, teachers reported great frustration about teaching the lower track. For one, this is due to the novel discipline problems. The classes do not respond well to traditional classroom management or teacher/content-centered teaching techniques. Teachers cannot rely on higher achieving 'draft horses' in their classes anymore and often feel unable to reach their teaching objectives. Some teachers questioned the whole system of tracking, but many more believed psychological support systems or retraining in a specific Hauptschule pedagogy may provide the answer. They are encouraged in this belief by some politicians and Western consultants. But we did observe lower-track classes which were taught in a student-centered way and where students participated and showed respect for and warmth towards the teacher. And yet, complaints were ubiquitous. Teachers led us to an understanding of this phenomenon during several in-depth interviews. East German teachers were used to cover a fixed amount of subject matter that was the unitary standard for all their classes. The heterogeneous composition of their classes allowed for a sufficient number of students to grasp the curriculum so that teachers could assume the appropriateness of the curriculum that was taught. The concentration of low achievers in one track requires of teachers to downgrade their curriculum, giving them the feeling that they, as teachers, had not done their job delivering the curriculum. This attitude reveals the teachers' strong sense of responsibility for the coverage of subject matter that they inherited from GDR times.

The classification, selection, and separation of — as one teacher put it — 'the dumbest of the dumb' in the general school who have little chance of success in the competitive labor market is a novel phenomenon for GDR teachers although special schools for learning disabilities did exist in the past and still do. Although tracking the 'lowest' students is accepted by many on philosophical grounds, out of social necessity, for the benefit of the school's reputation, or with a sense of a relatively immutable human nature, it seems to violate many teachers' sense of fairness and to strain teachers' sense of competence.

Summary

As their colleagues in the Gymnasien, many teachers in lower-track schools accept the reality of tracking, despite the lower status it entails for them, as a welcome alternative to the GDR experience or as fact of school life. They tend to identify their present school type with the former polytechnical school that was separate from the college-preparatory sphere in the extended secondary school. They contest, however, the present border between the college-prep sphere and their sphere of common schooling. In this regard the outlooks of educators at the non-college-prep Gesamtschule and the Regelschulen are similar. Teachers at the college-preparatory comprehensive school, on the other hand, appear to hold more mobility-oriented views.

While the power of the old school system in matters of curriculum standards and teaching routines is tangible, the traditional practice of inclusion has fallen victim to the new structural differentiation between lower and middle tracks and the ideological strength of the new meritocratic market society. While the institutional setting of the Regelschule in Thüringen is unequivocal with regard to issues of selection versus social integration, the Gesamtschule in Brandenburg is suspended between an inclusive philosophy or institutional charter and its lower status reality in the local school competition. This ambiguity produces frustration and defensiveness with regard to one's status among Gesamtschule educators. A novel phenomenon in all lower-track schools is the institutional production of a segregated at-risk student population. Here is a drama unfolding of which we have only seen the initial stages, and of which many Eastern German educators, having lived in a socialist society, are not yet fully aware.

Conclusion

Our study suggests striking similarities in policy and administration between the reform of the Eastern educational system and reforms of Western systems: ambiguous policies, a dearth of reform vision, loose coupling in pedagogical substance, but tight coupling in those basic elements of formal structure that align the system with the sorting mechanisms of the (Western) society.

State governments leave teachers largely alone in filling the new school types with life. In both states, a crucial source of educators' beliefs about their new school types is tradition, the past GDR school system, their own socialization experience, and routines of teaching practice. 'Apprenticeship of observation' (Lortie, 1975) in pedagogy demonstrates its power even under conditions of fundamental system change from above. Or perhaps, it is particularly strong precisely under such conditions since it serves to create certainty in a world that is changed by others. Yet it is rendered powerless in forging consistency between educators' beliefs and educational realities at the new work sites under conditions of fundamental change.

The New Structure of Secondary Schools

Overall, the 'conservative' Thüringen model seems to be more appealing and acceptable to educators in both states (an exception are teachers at the college-prep Gesamtschule in Brandenburg). There are several reasons why this may be so: the system is less ambiguous and thus avoids cumbersome competition among schools; it is more meritocratic and thus corresponds with the new successful economic model of the West; and it reproduces, at least in its design, the old split between the education for the masses and for the elite in the GDR. Given all three factors, it would not seem surprising if the other elements of the 'communist goal culture' (Lemke, 1991), social equality and inclusion, underwent further erosion. Whether that erosion is reversible remains an open question.

Notes

1 One may recall from chapter 2 that the Western school system consists of a separate elementary school, a lower-track Hauptschule, a middle-track Realschule, and an upper-track Gymnasium. In addition, comprehensive schools, incorporating two or three tracks, are more common in 'progressive' states. The GDR system consisted of a ten-year polytechnic school (POS) and a two-year college-prep extended secondary school (EOS).
2 As a result of state elections in the second half of 1994, the composition of both state governments has changed somewhat. In Brandenburg, the Social Democrats (SPD) gained an absolute majority and are now governing without a coalition partner. In Thüringen, the center-right coalition of CDU and FDP was replaced by a 'grand coalition' of CDU and SPD, with the CDU as senior partner. It is too early to tell the effects of these changes on educational policy. The observations in this book, in any case, refer to the governments in power through the later part of 1994.
3 A restructuring of the counties (*Gebietsreform*) has since been undertaken or initiated in almost all of the East German states, typically creating larger entities of county administration.
4 See Thüringer Kultusministerium (1991) *Vorläufige Lehrplanhinweise für Regelschule und Gymnasium*, Erfurt Verlag und Druckerei Fortschritt. For Brandenburg: Pädagogisches Landesinstitut Brandenburg (PLIB) (1992) *Vom Lehrplan zum Rahmenplan — PLIB Werkstattheft 1/92*, Ludwigsfelde, PLIB.
5 Evidence comes from participant observation as well as from a survey of the catalogue of central staff development centers: Thüringer Institut für Lehrerfortbildung (1992) *Fortbildungsprogramm für Lehrer(innen) und Erzieher(innen) im Land Thüringen*, Arnstadt, ThILLM. For Brandenburg: Pädagogisches Landesinstitut Brandenburg (1992) *Fortbildungsprogramm für Lehrerinnen und Lehrer im Land Brandenburg*, Ludwigsfelde, PLIB.
6 Note that total instruction time has decreased in some subjects (see chapter 3).

Chapter 6

Reproduction Versus Differentiation: The Politics of Higher Education

Institutions of higher education were of critical importance in the old East German order: they were designed to produce the leadership cadres for the state-socialist system of the German Democratic Republic (GDR), and their research was to a considerable degree oriented towards the state's needs for physical and social engineering and political legitimation. Access to them was highly regulated, and generally reserved to secondary school graduates who were seen as both academically able and dependably committed to the socialist order. Virtually overnight, this mission expired as the East German regime collapsed and its territory acceded to the Federal Republic of (West) Germany in the Unification Treaty of 1990. For the institutions of higher education in Eastern Germany, this marked the beginning of an extraordinary period of transformation which, on closer analysis, reveals a great deal not only about the specific situation of German higher education at an historical juncture, but also about the politics of higher education in a broader sense.

The ways in which the transformation of higher education in Eastern Germany has taken place (and continues to take place, as the process is by no means completed) represent some instructive variations on the politics of change in higher education. The project on which this chapter reports (and which is by no means completed either) has used this variation to shed more light on the nature of this process and on the political forces that it reveals. In a deliberate and somewhat exaggerated simplification, the principal dimension of variation is seen in the degree to which the reconstruction of higher education in Eastern Germany has followed, or sought to differentiate itself from, the model of higher education in West Germany. More pointedly, the question that we seek to answer is whether this reconstruction of higher education in Eastern Germany is more adequately described as an exercise in institutional 'cloning' or as an exercise in autonomous institutional development. The 'cloning' model would posit a substantial degree of conformity between the traditions, structures, and values of West German higher education and those of the new or reconstructed institutions of higher learning in the Eastern part of the country; the 'autonomous' or differentiated model, by contrast, would lead us to expect substantial differences between those two institutional profiles.

The main thesis of this chapter is that the prevailing tendency in higher education policy in the new *Länder* (states) of Eastern Germany is the reproduction of the existing system of higher education in Western Germany (substantiating, therefore, the 'cloning' model), but that there is significant variation in the degree to which this tendency manifests itself. This variation, it is argued, is at least in part explained by macro-political differences among the different political entities (*Länder*) that have been created on the territory of what used to be the GDR.

The chapter pursues this task by first providing some limited background information on the point of departure in this transformation process, i.e., the state of higher education in the old GDR, and on the overall direction of higher education policy in the five new Länder and in the Eastern part of Berlin. Against this background, we then examine several aspects of higher education policy in the new *Länder* — the legal framework, the role of the *Wissenschaftsrat*, the debate over new courses of study, and faculty recruitment — in an attempt to show how far, and through what means, the West German model has shaped the direction of policy in the Eastern part of the country.

Background

Higher Education in the German Democratic Republic (GDR)

For purposes of this exercise, there is little point in a detailed account of the system of higher education in the GDR. What should be useful, however, is a quick review of those features of that system that were of particular significance for the process of transformation following unification:

(i) The GDR adopted early on, and especially since the third reform of higher education in 1968, the Soviet system of a fairly rigid separation of higher education from the privileged research program of the *Akademien*. It was in the research institutes of the *Akademie der Wissenschaften* (AdW) that the bulk of research was conducted, in strict separation from the universities; the result was a substantial erosion of the research capacity of the universities in the GDR, accompanied by the migration of many of the best researchers from the universities to the *Akademien*[1].

(ii) Being thus relegated in large measure to teaching and training, the universities in the GDR had to carry the added burden of inculcating in the future elite of the country the principles of the country's reigning political paradigm. Thus, about 20 per cent of the teaching schedule, and a proportional number of staff, was devoted to instruction in Marxism-Leninism (ML), military education and sport.

(iii) Universities and other institutions of higher education in the GDR had a substantially higher ratio of staff to both the population at large and the number of students than was the case in West Germany. The difference was by a factor of at least two[2].

(iv) The percentage of an age cohort that was allowed access to higher education in the GDR was since the 1970s kept to a level of between 11 and 12 per cent through a fairly rigid *numerus clausus* mechanism that also channeled students predominantly into economically 'useful' fields like engineering, agriculture, teaching, etc., at the expense of the humanities, law, psychology and the non-applied natural sciences. This level compares to between 26 and 27 per cent in the former West Germany, and explains a substantial pent-up demand for university training in Eastern Germany upon unification (Wissenschaftsrat, 1992b, I, 6–7).

(v) Expansion of higher education in the GDR had been limited not only in terms of numbers of students, but also in terms of number of institutions. Here again, the contrast to former West Germany is striking, particularly where the development of *Fachhochschulen*[3] is concerned, of which in 1989 there existed ninety-seven in West Germany, and none in the GDR (Federal Ministry, 1992, pp. 68–9; cf. Wissenschaftsrat, 1991).

(vi) Lastly, and for obvious reasons, there was a substantial discrepancy in the content of university courses as between the two former Germanies. Notably in such fields as law, economics, education and most of the social sciences, the different social and political order of the GDR was reflected in the content of courses, the literature used, the examination requirements, etc. With the collapse of the GDR, the basis for much of this content disappeared in a number of fields, creating an enormous differential between fields of study as to the feasibility of continuing past educational practice and maintaining past curricula, literatures, and personnel.

Planning the Reconstruction

Even this brief sketch illustrates the extraordinary task that lay ahead as a unified Germany began to address the reconstruction of a system of higher education. This task fell, primarily, to two rather different sets of actors: On the one hand, the ministries of higher education of the newly emerging *Länder* in the Eastern part of Germany which, under the federalist division of labor of the former West and now all-German constitution, carry the principal responsibility for all matters educational, and the *Wissenschaftsrat* or 'scientific council', a body consisting of both distinguished academics and representatives of the federal and *Land* governments and designed to provide advice to those governments on major issues in higher education and research[4]. For a number of reasons, the latter of these two sets of actors, the Wissenschaftsrat, emerged as pivotal in shaping initial policy regarding the development of higher education in the Eastern *Länder*. First, in a situation where the newly-emerging *Länder* administrations were struggling to establish themselves as functioning bureaucratic organizations, the established advisory capacity of the Wissenschaftsrat assumed a particular significance as a dependable source of policy advice and direction, particularly for the federal government, but also for the planning commissions (*Strukturkommissionen*) for higher education set up in each of the new *Länder*. Secondly, it was clear that the massive task of reconstructing higher education in Eastern Germany, combined with the limited fiscal resources of the new *Länder* governments, required a major infusion of resources by the federal government, which has traditionally looked to the Wissenschaftsrat for guidance on how to allocate federal resources in the field of higher education and research. The tension which, in a number of critical areas, resulted from this dual and not necessarily consensual cast of characters became an important part of the politics of reconstructing higher education in Eastern Germany, and will interest us further later in the chapter.

In a truly colossal effort, the Wissenschaftsrat not only undertook the evaluation of the scientific establishment in the old GDR, but also went to work on a set of rather detailed recommendations regarding the reconstruction of higher education in the five new *Länder* and in East Berlin. The topics of these recommendations, compiled in four mighty volumes (Wissenschaftsrat, 1992b), range from the mechanisms for planning higher education in each *Land* to questions of recruitment and training or retraining of faculty and staff, and from the needs and directions of particular fields and disciplines to the assessment of particular institutions. Since the formulation of these recommendations, the Wissenschaftsrat has regularly monitored, and reported on, the compliance of the *Länder* with its recommendations; as of the middle of September 1992, as per the third such report, the Wissenschaftsrat found that 'the *Länder* have largely accepted the recommendations of the Wissenschaftsrat, and are implementing most of them. They have thereby paved the way for a fundamental renewal of the system of higher education in the new *Länder*' (Wissenschaftsrat, 1992c, p. 67). The reality behind this somewhat self-congratulatory statement happens to be, as we shall see, a good deal more controversial and contested.

The First Phase of Reconstruction

As of the end of 1992, the process of reestablishing a functioning system of higher education in the five new *Länder* and in the Eastern part of Berlin had made substantial progress. Since about the middle of 1990, planning commissions had been at work in each *Land* to assess the existing institutions of higher education and to design plans for revising, merging or closing them or for creating new institutions; many of these commissions had submitted their final recommendations by early 1993, and have proved to be an important link between the broader work and recommendations of the Wissenschaftsrat and the decision processes of each *Land* government. The work of these commissions would be worth a study in itself, particularly with regard to:

— their composition as a microcosm of the social forces that have a stake in higher education (academia, labor, business, research) and the resulting internal tensions;
— the struggle between shaping *Land* policy and legitimating decisions that had already been taken;
— the conflicts with the already existing institutions of higher education and their often entrenched academic and administrative establishment;
— the particularly thorny task of reconnecting the universities with the world of research (in the form of the successor institutes of the GDR Academy of Sciences); and
— the difficulty of serving, at least moderately, as a nucleus of innovation in a setting that was more inclined to adhere to 'tried and true' models of higher education.

As these commissions were still busy planning the future of higher education in their *Land*, the development or revamping of institutional arrangements in higher education proceeded apace; there were, after all, old and new students to be attended to, libraries, laboratories and other infrastructures to be maintained, and existing faculty and staff to be made use of. This parallelism of planning and actual development created problems of its own, especially where either individual institutions, relatively unencumbered by still fledgling ministerial bureaucracies, or *Land* ministries themselves went off in directions that were not at all in tune with the general direction that was shaping up in the Commission.

Reproduction Versus Differentiation

In terms of the institutional landscape and its development since 1989, the following summary observations can be made:

(i) Where universities are concerned, all new Länder have either maintained or slightly reduced their number of institutions, often through merging existing institutions; the exception is Brandenburg, which did not have a university-level institution in GDR times, and which has proceeded to create three new universities since 1989 (Potsdam, Frankfurt/Oder and Cottbus); the total number for the new *Länder* (including East Berlin) stood at twenty-eight in 1993, down from thirty-two in 1989 (Federal Ministry, 1992, p. 69)[5].

(ii) The center of activity in the creation of new institutions has been in the category of *Fachhochschulen* (see above), where a total of fifteen new institutions have been created between 1989 and 1993, with a number of additional ones scheduled to open over the next few years. This strong bias in favor of *Fachhochschulen* and in support of their more vocational, practice-related forms of study is consistent with, and a result of, the strong insistence by the Wissenschaftsrat, which has also been critical of Brandenburg for devoting so many of its limited resources to the creation of three new universities (rather than one, as the Wissenschaftsrat had originally recommended) instead of additional *Fachhochschulen*[6].

(iii) As these institutions continued or began their instructional programs, they underwent at the same time a substantial transformation in both their courses of study and the composition of their faculties. In both respects, this transformation is still in progress, although new curricula and examination requirements have by now been drafted or even implemented for a substantial number of fields. While this has been difficult and time-consuming enough, the task of filling the faculty vacancies that resulted from dismissal, resignation, or retirement of previous faculty or the creation of new positions has been similarly slow.

Institutional Cloning or Autonomous Development?

It would have been close to miraculous if a transformation of such magnitude and depth had occurred without any significant friction and conflict. After some initial debate, the decision had been made in early 1990 that the GDR and the (old) Federal Republic were to be united on terms that precluded any kind of amalgamation, but were predicated on the 'accession' of East

95

Germany to the territory as well as the legal, economic and political framework of West Germany. This being the case, the obsolescence of substantial elements of the pre-existing system of higher education in the GDR was essentially programmed, and the imperatives of both (relative) standardization within the new, larger polity and of relevance to an essentially West German system of economic production and social organization became the key premises for the new politics of higher education.

The Legal Framework

In legal terms, the principal instrument of standardization was the West German *Hochschulrahmengesetz* (HRG) (Framework Act for Higher Education) of 1986 (HIS, 1991, pp. 1–54) which, while leaving some room for variation across the *Länder*, draws a relatively narrow boundary around what is acceptable in terms of such key elements as courses of study, examinations and degrees, admission and, perhaps most consequentially, governance, where the 1986 law has largely taken back the somewhat more participatory arrangements that had been enacted in the wake of the student protest movement of the late 1960s. The room for departures from the West German norm in the direction of different kinds of degrees and different kinds of governance arrangements was thus very limited indeed; such room as there was available was, furthermore, interpreted somewhat conservatively by most of the agencies involved in the making of higher education decisions at both the federal and the *Land* level.

The Role of the Wissenschaftsrat

One of these agencies was the Wissenschaftsrat, whose critical role in masterminding the development of a new system of higher education in the new *Länder* of Eastern Germany cannot be overestimated. This role has to be seen in the context of the peculiar politics of federalism in German higher education where, even though the constitution clearly confers the ultimate authority in all matters educational upon the *Länder*, the federal government has secured for itself the position of a major player thanks to its fiscal resourcefulness. Under the terms of the *Hochschulbauförderungsgesetz* of 1970 (revised to reflect unification in 1990, see HIS, 1991, pp. 55–63), the federal government assumes the responsibility of covering 50 per cent of all investment costs in higher education — subject to a favorable evaluation of the investment projects by the Wissenschaftsrat. For the new *Länder*, all of which are struggling with the problem of grossly inadequate fiscal conditions, this provision assumed an even more critical role in the development of higher education than it did for the old *Länder* in West Germany, and made the Wissenschaftsrat an even more crucial judge in the assessment of each Eastern *Land's* projects for the development of a new higher education system.

Thus, when the Wissenschaftsrat, in January 1992, came to an unfavorable conclusion regarding the state of Thüringen's original plans to establish a 'European University' in Erfurt, the decision amounted effectively to the abolition of the state's plans, as Thüringen would not have been able to shoulder the substantial cost of building a new university out of its own meager resources (Wissenschaftsrat, 1992b, I, pp. 161–74)[7].

Other *Länder* dealt with the potential conflict between the *Land's* interest and the Wissenschaftsrat's nationally optimizing goals in different ways. A case in point is the state of Brandenburg, which sought ingeniously to pre-empt the *Wissenschaftsrat's* scrutiny by moving ahead with the establishment of three new universities, even though the Wissenschaftsrat, in its general recommendations, had strongly urged Brandenburg (as it had all other new *Länder*, except for Sachsen) to limit itself to one university only. Thus, when the Wissenschaftsrat finally got around specifically to assessing Brandenburg's plans for the development of higher education in the state, it was confronted with the *fait accompli* of three already existing universities (Potsdam, Cottbus, and Frankfurt/Oder) that could not very well be denied the badly needed federal subsidy.

One reason, incidentally, why Brandenburg insisted on defying the Wissenschaftsrat's proscription of more than one university in the state had to do with concerns over regional planning — a typical cause for disagreement between *Land* and federal assessments of a given project. In the case of Brandenburg, if the *Land* had been kept to one university, it would have most likely been located in Brandenburg's capital, Potsdam, right on the outskirts of Berlin. This would have left the relatively large hinterland of the state, and notably its eastern and southern parts, without any university — a situation quite detrimental to the development of these regions which were rather underdeveloped to begin with. Thus, from the planning perspective of the *Land*, it made eminently good sense to develop a wider network of institutions of higher education, and to place new universities in strategically important locations such as Frankfurt/Oder and Cottbus, rather than putting everything into a single location, notably one that was so close to the three already existing large universities in Berlin[8].

Thus, in the various controversies over what the Wissenschaftsrat recommended and what the individual *Länder* considered to be in their own best interests, the politics of federalism in German higher education reached another peak. Few of the new *Länder* have fully accepted the Wissenschaftsrat's recommendations, especially where the number and level of institutions were concerned. This is true especially with regard to the ratio between universities and *Fachhochschulen*: the Wissenschaftsrat's general persuasion for the new *Länder* had been to keep the university sector proper relatively limited while concentrating scarce resources for investment on the cheaper and more practice-related *Fachhochschulen* (Wissenschaftsrat, 1992b, II, pp. 45–144). This probably made sense as a rational strategy taking into account resource and labor market constraints; it underestimated, however, the political salience of using universities — existing as well as new — both as part of a regional development strategy and as a vehicle to assert the new *Länder's* claim to autonomous decision-making: on more than one occasion in many of the planning meetings, an irritated representative from one of the new Länder would raise the question of why the higher education policies of the old Länder were so much more easily taken for granted, while the new Länder had to accept a much heavier burden of proof for the adequacy of *their* policies.

Content and Courses of Study

Another domain where the new departure after 1989 could have generated some innovations, or some differentiation from the West German model, was that of the substantive orientation of university studies. Here, even pre-unification West Germany had been rife with criticism of the established order of knowledge production and transmission, particularly with regard to the humanities (*Geisteswissenschaften*), which were increasingly considered intellectually sterile and disconnected from some of the major intellectual challenges of our times (Frühwald *et al*, 1991). Here, where the existing legal frameworks would have presented no particular obstacle for innovation, and where the Wissenschaftsrat was occasionally even supportive of new programmatic directions, the yield of innovative elements in courses of study was, in fact, decidedly paltry. In university after university, the reconstruction of courses and programs of study followed the time-honored models of universities in West Germany. Exceptions are few and far between; they include such things as an environmentally oriented concept of engineering education at the Technical University of Cottbus, a joint institute for sociology and political science at the Humboldt University in East Berlin, a newly and differently conceived program of teacher education at the University of Potsdam, and an interdisciplinary department of comparative 'cultural studies' (*Kulturwissenschaften*) at the European University of Frankfurt/Oder. Especially the latter did and continues to encounter significant resistance from the German academic establishment, which expresses concern over the possibility that the interdisciplinary conception of the 'cultural studies' program might undermine the standing and integrity of the traditional disciplines[9].

Altogether, then, it appears that the opportunity to use the reconstruction of a sizeable number of universities as a veritable laboratory of educational and intellectual innovation has been largely missed — a conclusion also reached, with remarkable agreement, by a panel of German and American observers assembled at Harvard's Center for European Studies in the spring of 1992. The reasons for this overwhelming tendency to 'clone' the West German system of higher education in the East are probably many. They have to do with the dismal economic situation in Eastern Germany and the dearth of resources. They also have to do, however, with the replacement of a substantial portion of the East German academic personnel by academics from the West.

Faculty Recruitment

Probably the single most important indicator as well as cause of the remarkably 'reproductive' nature of the reconstruction of higher education in Eastern Germany is the mass migration of West German academics to take over key positions in the universities of the new *Länder*. The intensity of this migration, and the level of retention of East German academics, vary significantly across disciplines, reflecting the differential degree of susceptibility of different disciplines to the demands of the former East German state. The rate at which East German academics have been replaced by West Germans is thus highest — to the point of virtually an entire exchange of personnel — in the social sciences, law, education, economics, lower but still very significant in the humanities, and (relatively) lowest in mathematics, the natural sciences and engineering.

The discontinuation of East German academics was either accomplished through the closing of entire departments and the subsequent reopening and restaffing of similar departments ('Abwicklung') or through individual decisions based on one of two considerations: The person's lack of what were considered up-to-date and relevant professional and scientific qualifications, and their having compromised their academic integrity by close association with the agencies of the old regime. On one or both of these grounds, a substantial number of East German scholars were removed from their positions, and the ensuing searches for replacement tended to favor West German candidates. The reasons for this pattern appear to have to do with the following:

(i) The search committees appointed to fill professorial positions were overwhelmingly, and often exclusively, composed of West

German scholars whose networks of acquaintances, collaborators, and students were limited to West Germany, and who resonated much more to a style and language of presentation with which they were familiar;

(ii) Candidates from the former GDR (with the exception of those who were allowed to travel freely (*Reisekader*), which in turn made them subject to suspicion on political grounds) have an obvious disadvantage in that they are less likely to be as thoroughly familiar with the international (i.e., primarily Western) literature and research in their field than their West German colleagues;

(iii) At least some of the disciplines were eager to reproduce their 'schools' at the new universities in the East, which led to the notion and practice of *Seilschaften*[10] that are in some fields beginning to make the academic scenery in Eastern Germany look very much like a condensed version of what one might find in West Germany[11].

(iv) Since the number of professorships allocated to a given university or department would typically be rather small, a general sense on the part of the search committees prevailed that each appointment 'had to count' and that one could not afford the 'luxury' of appointing people whose professional standing was not fully recognized by their (West German) peers.

It is really quite extraordinary under these circumstances that at least some East German scholars did get appointed to social science professorships at universities in Eastern Germany. In fact, in those relatively rare cases where a special effort was made, rather impressive East German scholars were identified and appointed — even in disciplines as 'vulnerable' as political science and sociology.

Conclusion

These exceptions notwithstanding, however, the overall product of this process has been a system of higher education which, while still in formation, distinctly begins to look like a clone — or a wholly owned subsidiary — of West German higher education. This is remarkable for several reasons:

(i) the federal structure of the German policy system allows in principle for a substantial degree of variation across states, especially in education policy; this variation is curtailed or circumscribed by the federal *Hochschulrahmengesetz*, but by no means abolished;

(ii) periods of major social and political transformation should normally

be a particularly fertile ground for significant institutional innovation; this would seem to be especially true for the kind of change that has occurred in the Eastern part of Germany where, after the collapse of the GDR regime, almost everything had to start over again from scratch;
(iii) the West German system of higher education, which now finds itself cast in the role of model for what should happen in Eastern Germany, had been the subject of serious criticism prior to unification; instead of getting reformed, it is now being reproduced in the East[12].

While this overall degree of replication is indeed remarkable, it should be noted that there is significant variation across the different *Länder* (and, sometimes, even across institutions within the same *Land*) in the degree to which the West German model is accepted and reproduced. The single most critical factor in explaining these differences appears to be the configuration of political forces in the government of each *Land*: of the five new *Länder*, the one that has maintained relatively the most autonomy vis-a-vis the pressures for uniformity and federal regimentation in higher education has been Brandenburg, which is also the only one of the five *Länder* where a left-center coalition (SPD, FDP, *Bündnis 90*) was in power through 1994, while all others were initially governed by a center-right coalition headed by the CDU (Christian Democrats). Berlin represents an interesting intermediate position in that it is governed by a 'grand coalition' between Christian Democrats and Social Democrats, and could arguably be placed somewhere in the middle of the spectrum where the ease of accepting West German premises in higher education is concerned.

At the outset, this chapter posited two different models in the abstract for describing the process of reconstructing higher education in Eastern Germany in the aftermath of the collapse of the GDR regime: cloning or emulation and differentiation or autonomous development. Even with the variations noted, it seems clear that the situation we have described can hardly be seen as a serious effort at 'differentiating' between the West German and the emerging East German systems of higher education; with very few exceptions, such as Frankfurt/Oder, the direction is towards the incorporation of Eastern German higher education into the West German orbit rather than differentiation from the West German model.

Notes

1 The 120 institutes and 19,000 members of the GDR *Akademie der Wissenschaften* and its affiliates in the fields of agriculture and architecture were evaluated by

the German *Wissenschaftsrat* in 1990 and 1991. A substantial number of institutes and scholars were evaluated favorably, and their integration into universities or existing research organizations (such as the *Max-Planck-Gesellschaft*) recommended. See Wissenschaftsrat, 1992a; Kaiser, 1991; *Der Spiegel*, 27/1991; Bräutigam, 1991.

2   The GDR, with a population about one fourth that of West Germany, had a total of 38,000 academics at its universities, as compared to West Germany's total of 72,000; this difference is even more dramatic when related to the number of students (see next para.). Cf. Wissenschaftsrat, 1992b, I, 6.

3   Institutions to 'provide highly practice-related training for occupations which require the application of scientific findings and methods or artistic skills', offering study courses that are shorter than university courses, primarily for engineers and in the fields of economics, social work, computer science, agriculture, and design (Federal Ministry, 1992).

4   The members of the *Wissenschaftsrat* are appointed by the Federal President upon the recommendation of the major scientific bodies of the Federal Republic (the *Deutsche Forschungsgemeinschaft* as the principal research funding agency, the *Max-Planck-Gesellschaft* composed of the most prestigious research institutes, the assembly of the *Rektors* of German universities, and the special association of large-scale research facilities (*Großforschungseinrichtungen*)) and of the federal and *Land* governments; among the latter are also representatives of industry, labor, churches, and professional associations. They are joined by *ex-officio* representatives of the *Land* and federal governments.

5   The only addition since then has been the new University of Erfurt in Thüringen, officially founded in 1994, but still at the planning stage.

6   For comparison, the Western part of Germany (the 'old' *Länder*) had seventy universities and ninety-nine *Fachhochschulen* by the end of 1991 (Federal Ministry, 1992, p. 68).

7   As indicated above, the state of Thüringen, after much regrouping and redesigning, launched a new project for a university in Erfurt in 1994, taking the *Wissenschaftsrat*'s criticism of the earlier project into account.

8   The Brandenburg plan was not entirely driven by regional planning considerations either, however. It also foresaw a functional division of labor among the state's three universities: Potsdam with a special mandate for the training of teachers; Frankfurt/Oder as a 'European University' with a special mandate for linking the academic communities of Eastern and Western Europe; and the Technical University of Cottbus with a special commitment to Environmental Studies.

9   For a more detailed assessment of the Frankfurt (Oder) 'experiment', see Weiler, 1994.

10 Literally, a group of mountain climbers tied to the same rope; in this case, used to denote West German scholars who pulled their collaborators and students after them into faculty positions at the universities in Eastern Germany.

11 Including the major feuds that have been part of West Germany's academia for years; one search committee at a Brandenburg university managed to include the presidents of the two competing West German associations of political science.

12 The one part of former West Germany where, thanks to the political geography, both the reconstruction of East German higher education and the future of West German higher education became part of the agenda of the same political unit is Berlin. There, a reasonably serious effort was made not only to plan the new shape of higher education in the Eastern part of the city (notably the Humboldt University), but also to introduce some significant changes into the higher education system of (former) West Berlin (see Landeshochschulstrukturkommission Berlin, 1992).

Chapter 7

Educational Change and Social Transformation

In this final chapter, we will discuss certain aspects of the process of educational change in Eastern Germany that would seem particularly relevant for other educators who deal with the issue of educational change in their own countries. This broader interpretation of the Eastern German situation is based on the study's findings within the context of theories of educational change, and draws as well on our own experience as participant educators in the East German, West German and American societies.

We have characterized change in the Eastern German educational system as a process by which Western Germany imposes her organizational and normative principles on her socialist twin sister in the East so as to recreate national unity. Eastern German actors have little choice but to adapt to this institutional transformation. But the degree to which educators, parents, students, administrators and politicians are participants or mere objects in this imposition-adaptation configuration varies depending on the area of the educational system one looks at. While the reform of the state curricular frameworks was described as an instance of rather active appropriation of a Western model by consensual and participating Eastern educators, the remake of the universities, on the other hand, could best be grasped as an act of cloning, through which the West German system of higher education reproduces the basic characteristics of its own institutional identity in the Eastern part of the country.

Teachers, by and large, can be found between these two poles. They have to put up with, and adjust to, the decisions of politicians regarding the legal and formal structure of the system, to curricula that were composed by a select group of Eastern and Western educational professionals, and to the supply of textbooks made available by Western publishing companies. But they are at the same time given new freedom and responsibility in discharging their professional duties in schools and classrooms. This chapter takes another look at them and at the challenges they face. In doing this, we want to ask two questions: what kind of light does their situation and experience shed on the issue of systemic reform; and what insights, by looking at them,

Educational Change and Social Transformation

can we gain about the relationship between educational change and societal change at large.

Systemic Reform

In a certain sense, Eastern German secondary schools appear indeed to be in the throes of a rather encompassing effort of systemic reform. What we have observed and described in this book is an effort of political and administrative authorities to influence the practice and outcome of education by restructuring and reformulating key elements of the system so that the joint effects of these elements bring the personnel in the system to adopt certain desired patterns of behavior. In the Eastern German case, assimilation to the West, as the new dominant all-German national norm, requires the system to move in the direction of increasing democratization, differentiation, and individualization. The 'new' system emphasizes individual responsibility, self-actualization, selectivity, and competitiveness whereas collectivity, unitarianism, subordination, security and caring that were strong underpinnings of the old system are de-emphasized.

By comparison to the current American vision of systemic reform, the task at hand is enormous. Consequently, more parts of the system are targeted. The Eastern German agenda of total institutional remake indeed looks like a systemic reformer's dream. New laws and regulations stipulate the rights of all participants in the educational endeavor to codetermine the fate of the educational process in schools. New school types, whether stemming from the 'progressive' comprehensive tradition or the 'conservative' three-tier tradition, reintroduce tracking as a new feature in the early grades of secondary schooling. New state frameworks and approved textbooks are to prod teachers towards more autonomous instructional decisions and a more student-centered pedagogy. Rather substantial retraining programs are to support and sustain this development. With all of these levers in place, one really should expect schools to be on the move.

However, we observed varying degrees of success in these reform efforts. The chapters of the book demonstrate some of the reasons for the variation. While a systemic approach of sorts seems to have been a 'strength' of the past GDR order in which the authorities could speak with one voice, such a unified and integrated approach appears to be elusive under the new political conditions in Eastern Germany. We saw that already at the stage of policy formation, ambiguities, contradictions and inaccuracies in policy designs set in as soon as conflicting political interests are articulated.

We also showed how in the state of Brandenburg curricular frameworks, rooted in a common theme of mainstream 'progressivism', could be formulated and become law with rapidity. But the subject of 'ethics' was an exception in that it produced major conflict between the churches and the state. The ethics curriculum, therefore, was quickly declared an 'experiment' in order to contain the conflictual damage. Similarly, the new school types of which the new tracked school system consists are beset with design flaws that reflect the compromises struck in the political arena in both of the states we studied. These compromises revolve around the conflicting goals of mobility vs. status allocation, and of social integration vs. selectivity based on performance. These conflicts seem to be endemic in modern educational organizations, and are similarly reflected in the American debate about 'excellence' and 'equity'. Hence, the newly-installed school types in Eastern Germany turn out to be organizations in which 'institutional charters' and the defined structure of learning groups contradict each other or conflict with educational reality. The result is a lack of clear educational goals and mandates in those organizations, leaving the educational actors to wonder exactly what their schools' track status and appropriate pedagogy are supposed to be.

For the student of educational change this lack of coherence and clarity does not come as a surprise. The fundamental remake of Eastern German schools — within the boundaries of the Western institutional framework and of Eastern material and physical resources — could in theory have enabled reformers to pursue educational change with a grand plan of systemic reform in hand. After all, educational think tanks and experts from the West were available to serve the new authorities, and Eastern teaching personnel, caught off-guard by the demise of the GDR, was bewildered enough to be eager for new instructions. But rarely does the political process surrounding education produce such a coherent plan, nor do educational organizations lend themselves to the clarity in goals and structure on which systemic reform efforts are predicated. Urgent claims from researchers and reformers to the contrary notwithstanding, school reality is a fluid state of negotiation and compromise between conflicting goals and values that are rooted in social structural contradictions and human dilemmata. Eastern Germany is no exception to this regard; one encounters this negotiating mode not only at the level of political decision-making, but in each school faculty and each individual teacher. It accounts for the conspicuous vacillation and inconsistency in teachers' attitudes, beliefs, and actual practices that were detected in the studies.

The puzzle of forging a new educational reality is made even more perplexing by the initial weakness of the state governments and the scantness and abstractness of the legal and administrative measures with which the new ministries communicated their agenda to their subordinates. After all, forging formal-structural isomorphism with the West was paramount on the ministries' agenda. What sources can Eastern German teachers rely on in this type of reform for constructing a picture of their new school? In a worst-case scenario, the teacher consults the new school law that merely lays out the basic structure of the new school type. Or he or she peruses the new subject curricula that, by comparison to the old GDR syllabi, give orientation more by what they leave out than by what they actually prescribe as new teaching content. Newly-adopted Western textbooks follow their own curricular ideas, not necessarily corresponding to the state frameworks. In a best-case scenario, the teacher has had the opportunity to enroll in some in-service classes, or to visit some schools in Western Germany; and he/she is imaginative and competent enough to put the pieces together and construct his or her own vision of the instructional exercise. But in either case, teachers heavily borrow from their past experience and traditional assumptions in order to fill the gaps and make sense of the systemic markers that communicate the new institutional shell.

At the micro level of Eastern German schools and classrooms, the remake of the system is a daily trial and error affair. Here, teachers confront an amalgam of diffuse ideas of the new school and society, of traditional assumptions — stemming from schools and a society now vanished, but nevertheless still real in the imagination of people — and of the new character of their students. This character has changed due mainly to two things: the new structure of the school system has composed classes with unpredictable and unexpected learning and behavior potentials, and the transformation (*Wende*) generation of youth as a whole has adopted markedly different cultural traits and now claims and occupies more 'breathing space' in schools.

Thus, despite their broad scope, the administrative reform measures from above merely provide very indirect cues for behavioural change. These have powerful effects on teachers, but not necessarily the ones intended. For instance, by channelling students into certain tracks and learning groups, by allocating instructional time to these groups, by leaving it up to the teacher to find the appropriate treatment for them, and by extending students' and parents' rights, the new system forces teachers to face a new problematic reality, but does not offer specific solutions. As a result, teachers derive their principal orientation for teaching practice from the 'three As' of classroom teaching: achievement, appreciation and acquiescence, which need to be realized for the varied conditions of each classroom. In other words, teachers add to their repertoires what makes students learn, like them, and obey their rules — not necessarily in that order — neglecting the fuzzy 'big picture' in their deliberations.

Below the official façade of the school, the resulting teaching practice may or may not conform to official intent and rather often doesn't. Thus, we find college-prep schools with open admission where nobody fails, but everybody complains about their bloated state, and comprehensive schools that operate virtual dumping grounds to protect their higher-potential students; and we find the democratic intent of the new system reinterpreted in the daily interactions between politically abstinent teachers and supposedly defiant students. The situation in Eastern German secondary schools, then, illuminates in a particularly poignant way the difficulties of an encompassing systemic reform to induce the kind of change that policy-makers and state administrators intended.

Systemic educational reform travels at different speed depending on the element of the system that is targeted for change. The Eastern German case shows that laws can be decreed, organizations restructured, and even curricula reformulated in an incredibly swift manner when an unchallenged model is available towards which reforms are supposed to move. Even whole institutions, such as universities, can be recreated at a rapid pace when old personnel is discarded. But when educational change involves changes in the attitudes and behaviors of people, as in the case of democratizing and differentiating schools, then even far-reaching systemic reform comes slowly. The case of Eastern Germany reveals how attitudes and routines steeped in tradition are remarkably resistant to institutional change, particularly if it is imposed from above with little participation from crucial change agents at school sites.

Continuity and Change

The surroundings of the schools we studied are typical for the Eastern part of the country: areas of industrial decay, abandoned factory buildings, stretches of fallow land, and jobless men in the streets starkly contrast with shiny banking outlets, huge new shopping malls, an abundance of little sausage stands, and traffic gridlock. This contrast depicts the enormous economic plunge and restructuring towards Western capitalism which the Eastern part of Germany is undergoing; just as the noise with which the new political class articulates itself in the media is a conspicuous sign of the new pluralist political system. The restoration of Western property relationships is less visible. Its effect is not only that the formerly people-owned businesses are being privatized, but also that a sizeable number of ex-GDR middle class citizens are being expropriated or loose their homes, and that large numbers of tenants find their rented homes turned into somebody else's means of profit making. In the world of work, the challenges of change are manifold. A large number of East Germans are mastering the demands of a new job; many found work in the West or are enrolled in retraining programs. Many, however, altogether lost work as sustenance of identity, self-worth and income.

By contrast, schools endured through all these profound changes and, in the words of an administrator, 'did not even stop operating for a day' (apart from Saturdays which parents and students took off without asking). Nonetheless, all schools now have different school-type designations, most have newly-composed student bodies, faculties and new principals; all are directed by new state and local school administrators; all operate with new textbooks and copy machines, the latter probably the most profound technical innovation that was introduced to Eastern German schools as a result of the *'Wende'*. Schools are 'technologically simple and socially complex', as Michael Fullan remarks, and it is true that in the East German case, as well, the fate of educational change lies in that social complexity.

Not only did schools operate continuously when so many spheres of life were seriously disrupted, they also largely maintained continuity in their personnel. At first sight, it is surprising to an outside observer how the old GDR teaching force managed to stay almost intact through the transformation of communist party and state, and the subsequent unification process. Major personnel changes did not take place, even though the unity treaty between the GDR and the Federal Republic enabled the new authorities to lay off public servants, such as teachers; and even though the public reputation of the teaching profession as being responsible for ideological indoctrination and authoritarian deformation was at an all-time low. According to widespread public sentiment, many teachers had served the socialist state with 'anticipating obedience' until the very end.

Yet, when it came to the reshaping of the new school system, job security considerations could and did prevail over many others. This may have been so for a number of reasons. The GDR tradition of a guaranteed job, the new Western civil service rules, the principle of due process practiced by the new courts, and the general seniority assumptions of both teachers and administrators may have prevented a major personnel overhaul of the system. Besides, it is not clear to what extent beginning or unemployed Western teachers would have been available to fill openings. In any case, five years after the overthrow of the party regime, the teaching profession has closed ranks and enjoys substantial employment security. We encountered districts, for example, that would not hire a highly-qualified English or civics teacher from outside (i.e., often from the West) if they had teachers within the system who were willing to retrain for the sake of keeping their jobs while they already taught the subject. Understandably, the newly-formed personnel councils and unions support this policy. But in this way, the school system foregoes the chance of attracting 'new blood' and of benefitting from fresh impulses. While this practice may be expected from school districts in more stable environments, it is surprising for a school system that is ostensibly so committed to fundamental change. With job security and a relatively comfortable salary (that is still low compared with a Western teacher), teachers belong — relatively speaking — to the group of unification winners, particularly since so many teachers are female; and women's chances in the new labor market are considerably dimmer than men's. It is not surprising that teachers attach high priority to defending this economic position.

The two states we studied differ in the way they pursued personnel changes. In Thüringen, the Christian-democratic dominated state government purged the schools of high profile 'comrades' to a larger degree than the Social-democratic dominated government of Brandenburg where one can still find former party secretaries and principals as classroom teachers, sometimes at their original school sites. But the effect of these policy differences on educational change at these school sites is by no means clear. We do not (yet) have systematic data on this point, but we did observe at our sites in Brandenburg that a number of formerly high profile members of the 'Socialist Unity Party' had become very active and rather competent cadres in the current school reform. On the whole, the teachers we interviewed, whether formerly affiliated with the party or not, indicated that they in the past identified with socialist ideals and the GDR. The number of teachers in opposition to the system must have been very small if our study sites are any indication for the whole of the country.

If so much remained the same, what, then, has changed? This question is hard to answer because we do not reliably know what our research sites were like before the *'Wende'*. We therefore rely on general information about the GDR school system and foremost on our informants' testimony. We obviously need to be mindful that relying on their testimony may very well provide a distorted reflection of past reality. For we as outside researchers only become aware of those changes that teachers perceive as such and of those they are willing to admit. For a wide variety of reasons, certain changes seem to be downplayed in their importance and others, shrouded in silence.

Immediately following the political shift of 1989/90, teachers appear to have quickly jettisoned their attachment to socialist ideology and to have made a major effort of purging their language of those terms that might betray that attachment. Only in heated discussions or private conversations when self-control lessens do those terms, as a matter of habit, resurface in speech. Although there is no question but that teachers in GDR times played a key political role (representing the party's views, recruiting for the state youth organization and the army, and judging students on political grounds as much as on achievement), this role is often described in retrospect as a burden that was easily cast off.

The overwhelming majority of teachers with whom we had contact stress continuity over change with regard to their values and teaching styles.

Educational Change and Social Transformation

Now as before, they have been subject matter specialists at heart, and their teaching styles have been rather teacher-centered. Although one cannot exclude the possibility that stressing continuity may be a strategy to minimize deeds of the past, very few school teachers report dramatic internal personal changes related to their role as educators. The really major changes are perceived as coming from outside rather than inside the person. The new system and the new generation of students are the challenge.

Initially, the new system had to be 'swallowed' for the sake of saving one's job as a teacher. Thus, adaptation was a matter of survival, but it has been accomplished with a certain tangible reservation. Over the years, teachers have grown accustomed to the inevitable, and many have learned to take independent steps, some with remarkable activism and savvy. Yet, apart from the ideological distortions, many teachers doubt that their GDR schools were as bad as the (often Western) representatives of the new system and the media make them out to be. In the eyes of the teachers, schools in the bygone days of the GDR were more orderly and caring, content was more systematic, and students learned more although it is recognized that the GDR schools had to become more flexible in many ways. But the Western system is not necessarily seen as the convincing alternative. Here, teachers conform to public sentiment. Public criticism of the GDR past may have been stronger immediately after the collapse of the old regime, but three years after the installation of the new school system in Western fashion, a representative survey (see *Die Zeit*, 40, 1993, p. 20) reveals that 69 per cent of Eastern Germans consider the school system a particular strength of the former GDR; only 11 per cent think that the Western German school system is a particularly strong feature of the Federal Republic.

Skepticism towards school reform and a lack of identification and interpersonal involvement on the part of many educators is understandable if the present school reform fixes things that were not broken, especially when old practices — the political aspects excluded — were never experienced as problems, or if new 'solutions' imposed from above deteriorate the situation rather than improve it. It is indeed doubtful, for instance, whether running separate rock-bottom tracks for slow learners is much of an improvement over the integrated classes of the GDR school, especially for those schools and teachers that have to teach them. Yet, now that the integrated GDR school is lost, tracking has become rather popular among educators although it is not clear to what degree this change represents a true attitudinal modification and to what degree teachers merely execute the competitive dynamics of the new differentiated system.

The current school reform, regardless of political orientation of the state governments involved, is not a joint effort of concerned educational professionals, parents, and politicians in finding the best solutions for some identified problems, but the recreation of one school system in the likeness of another one with all its good and bad sides. Practitioners' reform efforts mainly consist of making the best of the new situation.

In the process, administrators are absorbed in organizational issues, while classroom teachers concentrate their reform activities on subject matter. This area comes under the joint purview of government and subject matter departments that need to interpret governmental will and design in-house curricula. Thus the area of teaching content — although the latter is dispensed in isolated classrooms — is a semi-public affair and therefore more accessible to political and administrative measures of state governments. Hence teachers' level of concern is high in this area.

Reforming teaching methods, on the other hand, is still on the back burner. This area is considered a deeply personal affair, and, indeed, it hinges upon a teacher's personality and style to a much higher degree than content. Schools are aware of the new message coming from staff development centers that the new state of the art pedagogy is student-centered, but experimenting with new methods of instruction requires a personal involvement in reform that many teachers lack. In addition, not all things can be changed at the same time, and instructional methods are an area where nobody at this point interferes or exercises pressure — almost nobody, that is. It is students who have slowly educated teachers by becoming more critical and by demanding more engaging, or simply refusing boring, instruction. Teachers, for the most part, are sensitive, if not as flexible, towards student demands. For, a certain degree of mutual distancing notwithstanding, students and teachers do engage in relatively close relationships. Eastern German secondary schools, even after the disruption of social bonds through the revamping of the system, are still warm and intimate places by comparison to an American high school. But some teachers, surely a minority of those we came in contact with, cannot find the key to the new *'Wende'* generation of students, particularly in lower-track schools. Those teachers harden and become ineffectual in their classes. At best, their lectures and demonstrations drone on while their students are off doing more interesting things in their minds; at worst they encounter serious discipline problems. This is not to say, however, that more student-centered instructional methods are a panacea for the plethora of social problems and emotional confusion that many present-day Eastern German students bring to class. The outcome of this adaptation process and the openness with which it is pursued by the individual teacher probably depends to a large measure on the collegial professional cultures to which the teacher is tied.

Does educational change come about more easily when it is embedded in large-scale societal change? We contend that the Eastern German case with its particular dynamic shows that this connection is not necessarily close, and that it varies for certain areas of the system. On the one hand, we can safely assume that the institutional remake of the entire system would have been less likely without the political and economic transformation. And this institutional remake affects every school and every teacher without exception, whether as willing participant or reluctant recipient. The latter group, much larger in number, appears to the observer remarkably untouched by the social transformation. Rather than being conducive to change, it seems that the scale and scope of societal change has created a blockage in many individuals that stems from tremendous insecurity, change overload, and stress. This blockage, although perhaps lessening over the years, is detrimental to learning and aggressive experimentation; it produces coping as the most widespread change strategy. One should not forget in this context that teachers are also parents and spouses, and even though their work situation may be relatively stable, living circumstances of the family are often not.

Eastern German schools, judging from our experience, have been transformed quite radically, but they are not hotbeds of reform despite or perhaps because of the tremendous societal changes that are going on around them. The missing element is a greater number of educators who reflect on the strengths and dark sides of the old school, are self-critical and competent about the new educational system and society, and present their views with self-confidence. Ironically the very success of a thorough institutional or systemic reform, in the context of a new and often disquieting societal order, has made less likely what is needed as an irreplaceable part in educational change: an empowered teaching force that is willing to embark on a course of conscious self-development.

Appendices

Glossary of German Terms

Abitur
  Secondary school leaving examination, usually at the end of grade 13 in the Gymnasium or the Gesamtschule
Abiturienten
  Graduates of the Abitur
Akademie (der Wissenschaften)
  Academy of Science of the GDR: Central agglomeration of research institutes, independent of universities
Bezirk
  GDR administrative unit between Kreis (county) and central government
Bildungsreform
  Educational reform, specifically the reforms of the late 1960s and early 1970s in the Federal Republic of (West) Germany
Bündnis
  Alliance of several groups associated with the democracy movement in East Germany, founded in 1990
CDU
  Christlich-Demokratische Union (Christian Democratic Union), principal conservative party in Germany
Deutsche Lehrerzeitung (DLZ)
  Leading professional magazine for German teachers
Die Grünen
  Green Party of Germany, with strong ecological orientations
Erweiterte Oberschule (EOS)
  Extended secondary school in the GDR, adding two more years to the ten years of POS, and leading to the Abitur at the end of grade ten
Fachberater
  Subject matter specialists serving as mentor teachers
Fachhochschule
  Special type of German post-secondary education institution, more vocationally oriented than universities
FDJ-Nachmittage
  After-school events organized by the communist state youth organization (Freie Deutsche Jugend, FDJ) in cooperation with the schools

FDP
: Freie Demokratische Partei (Free Democratic Party), smaller liberal party, currently in a coalition with the CDU in the federal government

Gesamtschule
: Comprehensive school, combining Hauptschule, Realschule, and Gymnasium tracks and designed as an alternative to the three-tiered traditional German school system

Gemeinde
: Municipality

Gesellschaftskunde
: 'Societal' or civic education, cf. Staatsbürgerkunde

Gymnasium
: The college-preparatory 'upper tier' of the traditional German school system, typically leading in nine years to the Abitur at the end of grade

Hauptschule
: The lower 'tier' of the traditional German school system (also known as 'Volksschule'), which is completed after five years at the end of grade nine

Hochschulbauförderungsgesetz
: Act (of 1970) to define the cooperation between federal and state governments in the funding of capital expenditures for higher education in Germany

Hochschulrahmengesetz (HRG)
: 'Act on the Framework for Higher Education', federal legislation of 1986 to provide a common framework for the organization of higher education in all states of the Federal Republic

Kreis
: County

Kreistag
: County assembly

Land (Länder)
: State(s) of the Federal Republic of Germany

Landrat
: County chief executive

Landtag
: State parliament

Lebenskunde — Ethik — Religion (LER)
: New subject in 'moral education' as an alternative to denominational religious instruction in the state of Brandenburg

Lehrplan
: Curriculum; curricular instructions for teachers

Lehrplantreue
: Adherence to curricular instructions

Glossary of German Terms

Leistungsgesellschaft
: Achievement-based society

Leistungsklassen
: Special classes set up for high-achieving students to enhance the internal differentiation of the GDR educational system

Leistungsprinzip
: Achievement principle

Max-Planck-Institut für Bildungsforschung
: Max Planck Institute for Educational Research, Berlin

Ministerium für Bildung, Jugend und Sport
: Ministry of Education, Youth and Sports (of the state of Brandenburg)

Modrow-Lehrer
: Personnel transferred from party and other political offices to teach in East German schools in the waning days of the GDR (under Prime Minister Modrow)

Pädagogisches Landesinstitut Brandenburg (PLIB)
: Curriculum development and teacher in-service training institution of the state of Brandenburg

Polytechnische Oberschule (POS)
: Comprehensive 'polytechnical' school (through tenth grade) in the GDR

Rahmenpläne
: Curricular guidelines (frameworks) for specific subject areas

Realschule
: The second or middle 'tier' of the traditional German school system, leading in six years to a middle-level certification ('mittlere Reife') that does not qualify for college admission

Regelschule
: 'Regular school', term used in the state of Thüringen to describe what is in essence a (vocationally oriented) Realschule, designed for all students not attending a Gymnasium

Restschule
: Term characterizing the Hauptschule as picking up the 'rest' or residue of students who do not qualify for either the Gymnasium or the Realschule

SED
: Sozialistische Einheitspartei Deutschlands (Socialist Unity Party), official state party of the GDR

SPD
: Sozialdemokratische Partei Deutschlands (Social Democratic Party), principal left-of-center party in Germany

Staatliche Schulämter
: Offices representing the (state) Ministry of Education at the local level

Staatsbürgerkunde
: Civic education

Stasi
: Ministerium für Staatssicherheit — GDR ministry for state security (secret service)

Statistisches Bundesamt
: Federal Office of Statistics

Strukturkommission
: Commission of experts set up at the state level to advise the government on the development of higher education in the state

Thüringer Landesamt für Statistik
: Office of Statistics of the state of Thüringen

Volksbildung
: 'People's education' — education sector in the GDR

Volksschule
: Older term for Hauptschule

Wende
: 'Turnaround', referring specifically to the political transformation in Eastern Germany (and other parts of Europe) in 1989

Wissenschaftsrat
: 'Scientific Council', joint advisory body of government and academic community for the assessment of plans for the development of institutions in higher education and research

Glossary of German Terms

Figure 1: Structure of the educational system of the (East) German Democratic Republic in the late 1980s

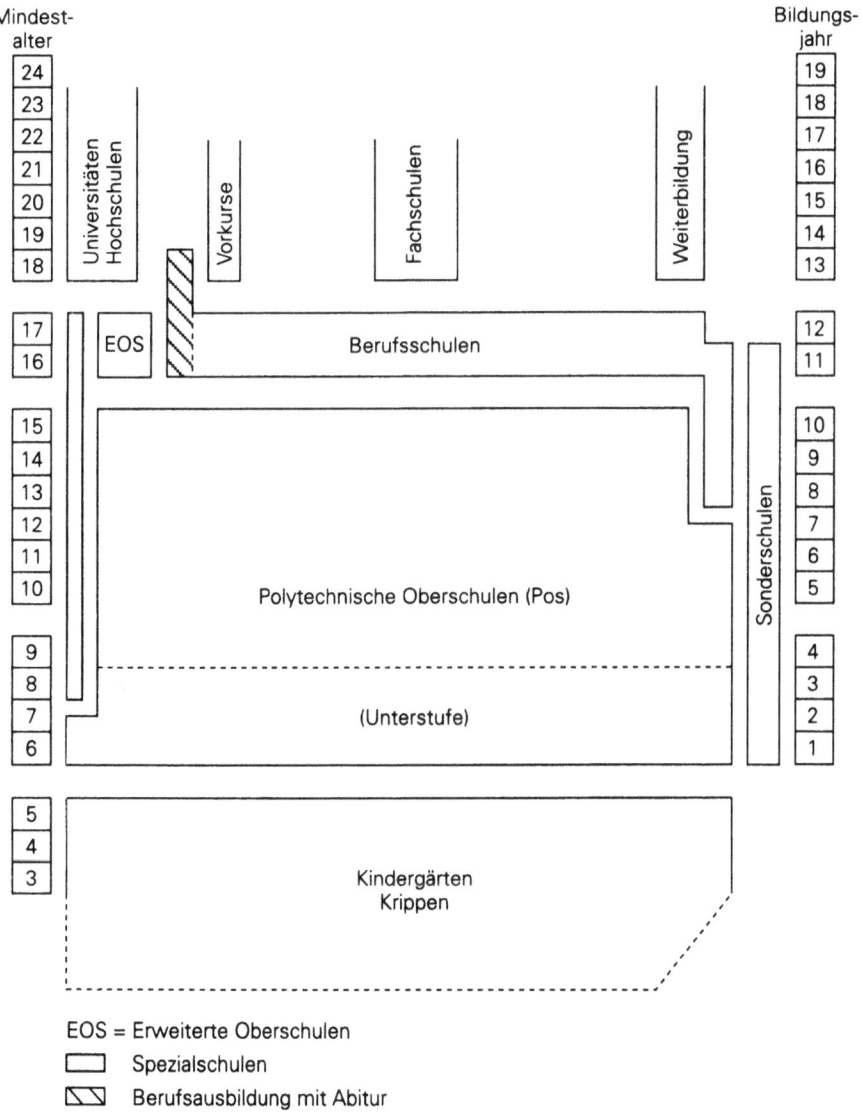

EOS = Erweiterte Oberschulen
☐ Spezialschulen
▨ Berufsausbildung mit Abitur

Educational Change and Social Transformation

Figure 2: Structure of the educational system of the Federal Republic of (West) Germany in the late 1980s

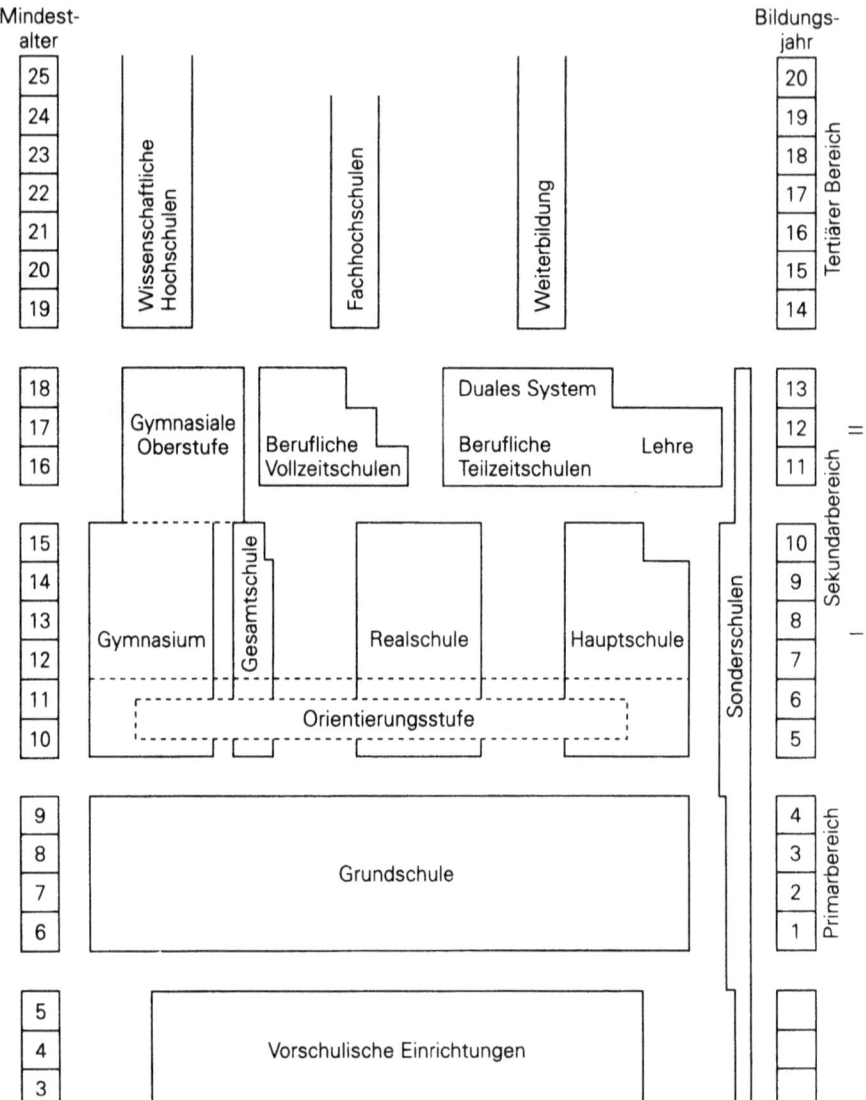

References

ABEND, V. (1990) 'Zur gegenwärtigen Erneuerung der Schule in der DDR', *Gymnasium Aktuell*, **2**, pp. 7–8.
ALMOND, G. and VERBA, S. (1963) *The Civic Culture*, Princeton, NJ, Princeton University Press.
ANWEILER, O. (1990) *Neue Entwicklungen im Bildungs- und Erziehungswesen der DDR*, Königswinter, Jakob-Kaiser-Stiftung.
BALL, S. (1981) *Beachside Comprehensive: A Case Study of Secondary Schooling*, Cambridge, Cambridge University Press.
BARR, R. and DREEBEN, R. (1983) *How Schools Work*, Chicago, IL, University of Chicago Press.
BASKE, S. (Ed) (1981) *Bildungsreformen in der Bundesrepublik Deutschland und in der Deutschen Demokratischen Republik*, Heidelberg, Meyn.
BERGER, P. (1991) 'Strukturbruch und Kategorienkonstanz — oder: Ein anderes "Verkehrssystem" für die fünf neuen Länder' in MEYER, H. (Ed) *Soziologie in Deutschland und die Transformation grosser gesellschaftlicher Systeme. Soziologentag 1991 Leipzig*, Berlin, Akademie Verlag.
BERNDT, I. (1990) 'Gesellschaftskunde statt Staatsbürgerkunde: Ein Etikettenwechsel?', *Pädagogik und Schule in Ost und West*, **4**.
Bildungsreform von unten: Materialien des Koordinierungstreffens von Vertretern bildungspolitischer Initiativgruppen, Berlin, 3. und 4. März 1990, Berlin, Unabhängiges Kontaktbüro Berlin.
BRÄUTIGAM, H. (1991) 'Notwendige Grausamkeiten: Rund 18,000 Forschern in den neuen Bundesländern droht das Aus', *Die Zeit*, 28 June.
BRENNER, M., BROWN, J. and CANTER, D. (1985) *The Research Interview*, London, Academic Press.
BROWN, A. and GRAY, J. (Eds) (1984) *Political Culture and Political Change in Communist States*, London, Macmillan Press.
BRZUKALLA, H. and HANSEN, R. (1982) 'Reformansätze in der Sekundarstufe II — Einstellungen von Lehrern und Schülern in bremischen Schulzentren' in ROLFF, H.-G., KLEMM, K. and TILLMANN, K.-J. (Eds) *Jahrbuch der Schulentwicklung. Band 2*, Weinheim and Basel, Beltz.
CARNOY, M. and LEVIN, H. (1985) *Schooling and Work in the Democratic State*, Stanford, CA, Stanford University Press.
COHEN, D. and BALL, D. (1990) 'Policy and practice: An overview', *Educational Evaluation and Policy Analysis*, **12**, 3, pp. 347–53.

CUBAN, L. (1990) 'Reforming again, again, and again', *Educational Researcher*, **19**, 1, pp. 3–13.
CUBAN, L. (1992) 'Curriculum stability and change' in JACKSON, P. (Ed) *Handbook of Research on Curriculum*, New York, Macmillan.
DALTON, R. (1991) *'Politics in the New Germany'* (paper), Irvine, CA, University of California.
Der Spiegel (1991) 'Ihr habt viele niedergemäht', 27.
DREEBEN, R. and BARR, R. (1988) 'Classroom composition and the design of instruction', *Sociology of Education*, **61**, 3, pp. 129–42.
DREWELOW, H. (1990) 'Für ein verändertes Lehrplanverständnis', *Pädagogik*, **45**, 3, pp. 197–201.
ELMORE, R. and SYKES, G. (1992) 'Curriculum stability and change' in JACKSON, P. (Ed) *Handbook of Research on Curriculum*, New York, Macmillan.
Federal Ministry of Education and Science (1992) *Basic and Structural Data: Education Statistics for the Federal Republic of Germany, 1992/93*, Bonn, Federal Ministry of Education and Science.
FEND, H. (1977) *Schulklima: Soziale Einflußprozesse in der Schule*, Weinheim, Beltz.
FETTERMAN, D. (1989) *Ethnography Step by Step*, Newbury Park, Sage.
FINLEY, M. (1984) 'Teachers and tracking in a comprehensive high school', *Sociology of Education*, **57**, October, pp. 233–43.
FISCHER, A. (1992) *Das Bildungssystem der DDR: Entwicklung, Umbruch, und Neugestaltung seit 1989*, Darmstadt, Wissenschaftliche Buchgesellschaft.
FISHMAN, S. and MARTIN, L. (1987) *Estranged Twins*, New York, Praeger.
FRIEDEBURG, L.v. (1992) *Bildungsreform in Deutschland*, Frankfurt am Main, Suhrkamp.
FRÜHWALD, W. et al. (1991) *Geisteswissenschaften heute: Eine Denkschrift*, Frankfurt/Main, Suhrkamp.
FUHRMAN, S., CLUNE, W. and ELMORE, R. (1988) 'Research on education reform: Lessons on implementation of policy', *Teachers College Record*, **90**, 2, pp. 237–58.
FULLAN, M. (1991) *The New Meaning of Educational Change*, New York, Teachers College Press.
GEISSLER, R. (1990) 'Bildungschancen in der DDR — Erfolge und Misserfolge sozialistischer Bildungsplanung', *Grundlagen der Weiterbildung*, **1**, 1, pp. 8–9.
GIESEN, B. and LEGGEWIE, K. (Eds) (1991) *Experiment Vereinigung*, Berlin, Rotbuch.
Große DLZ-Umfrage (1990) 'Die DDR-Länder sind im Kommen. Auch ihre Schulen', *Deutsche Lehrerzeitung*, **33**, pp. 4–5.
GRUNER, P. (Ed) (1990) *Angepasst oder mündig. Briefe an Christa Wolf im Herbst 1989*, Frankfurt/M, Luchterhand.
GUTTMANN, A. (1987) *Democratic Education*, Princeton, NJ, Princeton University Press.
HABEL, W., HANSEN, R., KRAMPE, C., PORTZ, S. and SPIES, W. (1992) 'Das Gymnasium zwischen Bildungsprogrammen und Realität' in ROLFF, H.-G. (Ed) *Jahrbuch der Schulentwicklung. Band 7*, Weinheim, Juventa.
HALLINAN, M. and SORENSEN, A. (1983) 'The formation and stability of instructional groups', *American Sociological Review*, **48**, pp. 838–51.

References

HEARNDEN, A. (1974) *Education in the Two Germanies*, Oxford, Blackwell.
HEINRICH, H. (1990) 'Wie weiter mit den Leistungsklassen', *Pädagogik*, **45**, 10, pp. 761–8.
HEMMINGS, A. and METZ, M. (1990) 'Real teaching: How high school teachers negotiate societal, local community, and student pressures when they define their work' in PAGE, R. and VALLI, L. (Eds) *Interpretive Studies in US Secondary Schools*, Albany, NY, State University of New York Press.
HENTIG, H.v. (1990) 'Geduld für den Wandel', *Die Zeit*, **47**.
HIS — Hochschul-Informations-System GmbH (1991) *Hochschulrahmengesetz — Hochschulbauförderungsgesetz — Landesrecht für die neuen Bundesländer*, Hannover, HIS.
HUBERMAN, M. and MILES, M. (1984) *Innovation up Close*, New York, Plenum.
KAACK, H. (1990) 'Gesamtschule und/oder gegliedertes Schulsystem', *Deutsche Lehrerzeitung*, 39/90, pp. 13–14.
KAISER, J. (1991) 'Nach den Gutachten: Gemischter Befund, schlechte Aussichten', *Der Tagesspiegel*, 7 July.
KEDDIE, N. (1971) 'Classroom knowledge' in YOUNG, M. (Ed) *Knowledge and Control*, London, Collier-Macmillan.
KIEFER, P. (1990) 'Lippenbekenntnisse nein, aber . . .' *Pädagogik*, **45**, 10, pp. 791–3.
KIENITZ, V. (1990) 'Zur Weiterentwicklung des Verhältnisses von Einheitlichkeit und Differenziertheit', *Pädagogik*, **45**, 2, pp. 105–12.
KLEMM, K., BÖTTCHER, W. and WEEGEN, M. (1992) *Bildungsplanung in den neuen Bundesländern*, Weinheim and München, Juventa.
KLIER, F. (1990) *Lüg Vaterland. Erziehung in der DDR*, München, Kindler.
KÖNIG, H.J. (1990) 'Schulreform im Aufwind der Föderalisierung', *Deutsche Lehrerzeitung*, **4**, p. 10.
KRIESEL, A. (1993) *Zur Begründung für den neuen Lernbereich 'Lebensgestaltung/Ethik/Religion': Die Situation der Heranwachsenden* (PLIB-Werkstattheft), Ludwigsfelde, PLIB.
KUEHNEL, W. and HEITMEYER, W. (1991) ' "Doppelte Identität" zwischen offizieller Norm und eigener Erfahrung', *Frankfurter Rundschau Dokumentation*, 10 July, p. 8 (Vorabdruck eines Beitrages in 'Blätter für deutsche und internationale Politik' Oktober 1991).
LACEY, C. (1970) *Hightown Grammar. The School as a Social System*, Manchester, Manchester University Press.
Landeshochschulstrukturkommission Berlin (1992) *Stellungnahmen und Empfehlungen zu Struktur und Entwicklung der Berliner Hochschulen*, Berlin, Landeshochschulstrukturkommission.
LEMKE, C. (1991) *Die Ursachen des Umbruchs 1989. Politische Sozialisation in der ehemaligen DDR*, Opladen, Westdeutscher Verlag.
LEPENIES, W. (1992) *Folgen einer unerhörten Begebenheit: Die Deutschen nach der Vereinigung*, Berlin, Siedler.
LITTLE, J. (1993) 'Professional community in comprehensive high schools: The two worlds of academic and vocational teachers' in LITTLE, J. and McLAUGHLIN, M.

(Eds) *Teachers' Work. Individuals, Colleagues, and Contexts*, New York, Teachers College Press.
LITTLE, J. and MCLAUGHLIN, M. (Eds) (1993) *Teachers' Work. Individuals, Colleagues, and Contexts*, New York, Teachers College Press.
LORTIE, D. (1975) *Schoolteacher*, Chicago, IL, University of Chicago Press.
MCLAUGHLIN, M. (1990) 'The Rand change agent study revisited: Macro perspectives and micro realities', *Educational Researcher*, **19**, 9, pp. 11–16.
MCLAUGHLIN, M. and TALBERT, J. (1993) 'Contexts that matter for teaching and learning', Stanford, Center for Research on the Context of Secondary School Teaching (unpublished paper).
MARSH, D. and ODDEN, A. (1991) 'Implementation of the California mathematics and science curriculum frameworks' in ODDEN, A. (Ed) *Education Policy Implementation*, Albany, NY, SUNY Press.
MEIER, A. (1990) 'Abschied von der sozialistischen Ständegesellschaft', *Aus Politik und Zeitgeschichte. Das Parlament* Nr. B 16–17, pp. 3–14.
METZ, M. (1990) 'How social class differences shape teachers' work' in MCLAUGHLIN, M., TALBERT, J. and BASCIA, N. (Eds) *The Contexts of Teaching in Secondary Schools*, New York, Teachers' College Press.
MEUMANN, E. (1990) 'Herausforderungen und Chancen für Erziehung', *Pädagogik*, **45**, 1, pp. 19–29.
MEYER, H.J. (1990) 'Die humane Mitte im Spannungsfeld von Leistung und Solidarität', *Deutsche Lehrerzeitung*, **35**/90, p. 1.
MEYER, J. (1977) 'The effects of education as an institution', *American Journal of Sociology*, **83**, pp. 55–77.
MEYER, J. and ROWAN, B. (1977) 'Institutionalized organizations: Formal structure as myth and ceremony' in MEYER, J. and SCOTT, W.R. (Eds) *Organizational Environments*, Beverly Hills, CA, Sage.
MEYER, J. and ROWAN, B. (1978) 'The structure of educational organizations' in MEYER, J. and SCOTT, W.R. (Eds) *Environments and Organizations*, San Francisco, CA, Jossey-Bass.
Ministerium für Bildung, Jugend und Sport, Brandenburg (1991) *Erstes Schulreformgesetz für das Land Brandenburg*, Potsdam, MBJS.
Ministerium für Bildung, Jugend und Sport, Brandenburg (1992a) *Schule im Land Brandenburg*, Potsdam, MBJS.
Ministerium für Bildung, Jugend und Sport, Brandenburg (1992b) *Vorläufige Daten aus dem Schulbereich*, unpublished, MBJS.
Ministerium für Bildung, Jugend und Sport, Brandenburg (1992c) *Aufbauprogramm Brandenburg*, unpublished, MBJS.
MINTROP, H. and WEILER, H. (1993) 'Democratization from above or below: The state and the teachers in Eastern Germany', paper presented at the annual meeting of the American Educational Research Association, Atlanta, April.
MINTROP, H. and WEILER, H. (1994) 'The relationship between educational policy and practice: The reconstitution of the college-preparatory gymnasium in East Germany', *Harvard Educational Review*, **64**, 3, Fall, pp. 247–77.
MITTER, W. (1981) 'Gesamtschulen in der Bundesrepublik Deutschland und die

References

Allgemeine polytechnische Oberschule der DDR. Kriterien für einen Vergleich (Skizze)' in BASKE, S. (Ed) *Bildungsreformen in der Bundesrepublik Deutschland und in der Deutschen Demokratischen Republik*, Heidelberg, Meyn, pp. 9–24.

MITTER, W. (1992) 'Educational adjustments and perspectives in a united Germany', *Comparative Education,* **28**, 1, pp. 45–52.

MOSTYN, B. (1985) 'The content analysis of qualitative research data: A dynamic approach' in BRENNER, M., BROWN, J. and CANTER, D. (Eds) *The Research Interview: Uses and Approaches*, New York, Academic Press.

MÜLLER, B. (1990) 'Weg vom "alten Stiefel" der Einheitsschule', *Deutsche Lehrerzeitung*, **32**/90, p. 3.

OAKES, J. (1985) *Keeping Track. How Schools Structure Inequality*, New Haven, CT, Yale University Press.

OAKES, J., GAMORAN, A. and PAGE, R. (1992) 'Curriculum differentiation: Opportunities, outcomes, and meanings' in JACKSON, P. (Ed) *Handbook of Research on Curriculum*, Washington, DC, American Educational Research Association.

Oberschule 'Alfred Kurella' (1990) 'Der Lehrer im pädagogischen Alltag' (Gespräch), *Pädagogik*, **45**, 1, pp. 41–5.

O'DONNELL, G. and SCHMITTER, P. (1986) *Transitions from Authoritarian Rule*, Baltimore, MD, Johns Hopkins University Press.

OFFE, C. (1991) 'Prosperity, nation, republic: Aspects of the unique German journey from socialism to capitalism', *German Politics and Society*, **22**, spring, pp. 18–32.

OKUN, B. (1990) 'Wider die Schere im Kopf' (interview), *Pädagogik*, **45**, 4, pp. 273–6.

OSWALD, H., BAKER, D. and STEVENSON, D. (1988) 'School charter and parental management in West Germany', *Sociology of Education*, **61**, 4, pp. 255–65.

Pädagogisches Landesinstitut Brandenburg (PLIB) (1992) *Vom Lehrplan zum Rahmenplan: Arbeitsmaterialien zur Unterrichtsreform im Land Brandenburg* (PLIB-Werkstattheft 1/92), Ludwigsfelde, PLIB.

Pädagogisches Zentrum (Ed) (1990/91) *Informationen zum Bildungswesen der Neuen Bundesländer* (issues 3 (1990) and 1 (1991)), Berlin, PZ.

PAGE, R. and VALLI, L. (Eds) (1990) *Curriculum Differentiation: Interpretive Studies in US Secondary Schools*, Albany, NY, SUNY Press.

PHILIPP, E. and WITJES, W. (1982) 'Gymnasium — Abkehr von der Standesschule?' in ROLFF, H.-G., KLEMM, K. and TILLMANN, K.-J. (Eds) *Jahrbuch der Schulentwicklung. Band 2*, Weinheim and Basel, Beltz.

POLLACK, D. (1990) 'Das Ende einer Organisationsgesellschaft: Systemtheoretische Überlegungen zum gesellschaftlichen Umbruch in der DDR', *Zeitschrift für Soziologie*, **19**, 4, pp. 292–307.

RIST, R. (1977) 'On understanding the processes of schooling' in KARABEL, J. and HALSEY, A. (Eds) *Power and Ideology in Education*, New York, Oxford University Press.

RÖHRS, H. (Ed) (1969) *Das Gymnasium in Geschichte und Gegenwart*, Frankfurt/M, Akademische Verlagsgesellschaft.

ROLFF, H.-G. (1992) 'Krise der Schulstruktur', *Pädagogik*, 2/92, pp. 38–41.

ROSENHOLTZ, S. (1991) *Teachers' Workplace: The Social Organization Of Schools*, New York, Teachers' College Press.
RUDOLF, R. (1990) 'Was ist das wirklich, Erziehung?', *Pädagogik*, 45, 12, pp. 914–21.
SARASON, S.B. (1982) *The Culture of the School and the Problem of Change*, Boston, MA, Allyn and Bacon.
SARASON, S.B. (1990) *The Predictable Failure of Educational Reform: Can We Change Course Before It's Too Late?* San Francisco, Jossey-Bass.
SCHMIDT, G. (1990) 'Bildungsreform in der DDR — Grundlegende Erneuerung der Schule?', *Forum E*, 2/90, pp. 9–12.
SCHMIDT, W. (1991) *Lehrerüberprüfungen und Stellenreduzierungen in den neuen Bundesländern*, Berlin, Gesamtdeutsches Institut.
SCHREINER, G. (1991) 'Undemokratischer Schulalltag? — Vergleichende Erkundungen in Ost- und Westdeutschland', *Zeitschrift für Internationale Erziehungs- und Sozialwissenschaftliche Forschung*, 8, 2, pp. 243–77.
SCHREINER, M. (1990) 'Kopieren ist kein Neubeginn', *Forum E*, 2/90, p. 13.
SCHWERIN, E. (1990) 'Die Bildungsreform in der DDR als gesamtgesellschaftlicher Prozeß', *Pädagogik und Schule in Ost und West*, 2/1990, 73f.
SCHWILLE, J., et al. (1988) 'State policy and the control of curriculum decisions', *Educational Policy*, 2, 1, pp. 29–50.
SORENSEN, A. (1970) 'Organizational differentiation of students and educational opportunity', *Sociology of Education*, 43, Fall, pp. 355–76.
Statistisches Bundesamt (1992) *Statistisches Jahrbuch für die Bundesrepublik Deutschland*, Wiesbaden, Metzler-Poeschel.
STEFFENS, U. and BARGEL, T. (1993) *Erkundungen zur Qualität von Schule*, Neuwied, Luchterhand.
TALBERT, J. (1990) 'Teacher tracking: Exacerbating inequalities in the high school' Stanford, CA, Center for Research on the Context of Secondary Teaching (unpublished paper).
TALBERT, J. and MCLAUGHLIN, M. (1993) 'Understanding teaching in context' in COHEN, D., MCLAUGHLIN, M. and TALBERT, J. (Eds) *Teaching for Understanding*, San Francisco, CA, Jossey-Bass.
Thüringer Kultusministerium (1991a) *Vorläufiges Bildungsgesetz*, Erfurt, TKM.
Thüringer Kultusministerium (1991b) *Vorläufige Schulordnung für die Regelschule*, Erfurt, TKM.
Thüringer Kultusministerium (1992a) *Thüringer Gesetz über die Finanzierung der staatlichen Schulen*, Erfurt, TKM.
Thüringer Kultusministerium (1992b) *Die schulischen Bildungswege in Thüringen*, Erfurt, TKM.
Thüringer Landesamt für Statistik (1992) *Die allgemeinbildenden Schulen in Thüringen 1991. Statistischer Bericht*, Erfurt, TLS.
TIEFENSEE, E. (1990) 'Religionsunterricht an der Schule? Die DDR-Situation ist einmalig', *Pädagogik und Schule in Ost und West*, 3/1990, p. 189f.
TILLMANN, K.-J. (1990) 'Die Schulentwicklung in der Bundesrepublik Deutschland und der Blick auf die Reformdiskussion in der DDR', *Vergleichende Pädagogik*, 26, 2, pp. 113–25.

References

UHLIG, G. (Ed) (1970) *Dokumente zur Geschichte des Schulwesens in der Deutschen Demokratischen Republik*, Monumenta Paedagogica, Berlin, Volk und Wissen.

VON BEYME, K. (1991) *Das politische System der Bundesrepublik Deutschland nach der Vereinigung*, München, Piper.

WATERKAMP, D. (1987) *Handbuch zum Bildungswesen der DDR*, Berlin, Spitz.

WATERKAMP, D. (1990) 'Schule in der DDR — eine Bilanz' in ROLFF, H.-G. et al. (Eds) *Jahrbuch der Schulentwicklung, Band 6*, Weinheim, Juventa.

WEATHERLY, R. (1979) *Reforming Special Education: Policy Implementation from State Level to Street Level*, Cambridge, MIT Press.

WEICK, K. (1976) 'Educational organizations as loosely coupled systems', *Administrative Science Quarterly*, **21**, March, pp. 1–19.

WEICK, K. (1982) 'Management of organizational change among loosely coupled elements' in GOODMAN, P. et al. (Eds) *Change in Organizations*, San Francisco, Jossey-Bass.

WEILER, H. (1983) 'Legalization, expertise, and participation: Strategies of compensatory legitimation in educational policy', *Comparative Education Review*, **27**, 2, June, pp. 259–77.

WEILER, H. (1989) 'Why reforms fail: The politics of education in France and the Federal Republic of Germany', *Journal of Curriculum Studies*, **21**, 4, pp. 291–305.

WEILER, H. (1990) 'Curriculum reform and the legitimation of educational objectives: The case of the Federal Republic of Germany', *Oxford Review of Education*, **16**, 1, pp. 15–27.

WEILER, H. (1993) 'Control versus legitimation: The politics of ambivalence' in HANNAWAY, J. and CARNOY, M. (Eds) *Decentralization and School Improvement*, San Francisco, CA, Jossey-Bass.

WEILER, H. (1994) 'Conceptions of knowledge and institutional realities: Reflections on the creation of a new university in Eastern Germany', *Oxford Review of Education*, **20**, 4, pp. 429–40.

WEILER, H. and MINTROP, H. (1992) 'The scale of governance and the micropolitics of educational change: Education and politics in the new Germany', paper presented at the annual meeting of the American Educational Research Association, San Francisco, April.

WERNSTEDT, R. and SCHITTKO, K. (1991) *Die deutsche Einheit unter der Perspektive der Gesamtschulentwicklung*, Beitrag für die Gesamschulinformationen des PZ, Berlin, Pädagogisches Zentrum.

WIRT, F. and KIRST, M. (1989) *Schools in Conflict*, Berkeley, CA, McCutchan.

Wissenschaftsrat (1991) *Empfehlungen zur Entwicklung der Fachhochschulen in den 90er Jahren*, Köln, Wissenschaftsrat.

Wissenschaftsrat (1992a) *Stellungnahmen zu den außeruniversitären Forschungseinrichtungen der ehemaligen DDR* (10 vols), Köln, Wissenschaftsrat.

Wissenschaftsrat (1992b) *Empfehlungen zur künftigen Struktur der Hochschullandschaft in den neuen Ländern und im Ostteil von Berlin, Teil I–II*. Köln, Wissenschaftsrat.

Wissenschaftsrat (1992c) *Dritter Bericht zum Stand der Umsetzung der Empfehlungen des Wissenschaftsrates an den Hochschulen der neuen Länder* (Drs. 893/92), Köln, Wissenschaftsrat.

YIN, R. (1989) *Case Study Research. Design and Methods*, Newbury Park, CA, Sage.

ZAPF, W. (1991) 'Der Untergang der DDR und die soziologische Theorie der Modernisierung' in GIESEN, B. and LEGGEWIE, K. (Eds) *Experiment Vereinigung*, Berlin, Rotbuch, pp. 38–51.

ZAPF, W. (1992) 'Die Transformation in der ehemaligen DDR und die soziologische Theorie der Modernisierung' Gastvortrag. Max-Planck-Institut für Gesellschaftsforschung, *Discussion Paper*, **92**/4, Köln, MPIFG.

Index

Abend, V. 19
ability grouping 72, 75–6
Abitur 9, 10, 14
achievement 26, 71, 75
administration 60–62, 66–7, 71
Almond, G. and Verba, S. 4, 37
anti-fascism 12–13
Anweiler, O. 8
apprenticeships 9, 10, 73
astronomy 34

Baske, S. 8
Berlin Wall 1, 14
Berndt, I. 26
Birthler, Marianne 28
Brandenburg
  adoption of three-tier secondary schools 30, 58–60, 66
  acceptance of tracking 71–4
  government agencies 60–62, 66–7, 71
  lower track schools 84–8
  proposed *Hauptschule* 85
  status of the *Gesamtschule* 64–6, 69, 70, 82–4, 85–6, 88
  status of the *Gymnasium* 74–81
  curriculum reform 22–4
  assimilation versus differentiation 35–6
  chemistry 32
  departure from GDR traditions 24–5
  foreign language teaching 26, 27–8
  Gesellschaftskunde (societal education) 25–6
  Lebenskunde-Ethik-Religion (LER) 32, 33, 106
  Leistungsklassen (achievement classes) 26
  new subjects 32, 33
  philosophy 32–3
  public consultation 27–8
  religious instruction 28
  school week 26, 27
  subject matter frameworks 30–31, 34
  teacher training 34–5
  traditional subjects 31–2

first state elections 28
new universities 97
Pädagogisches Landesinstitut (PLIB) 29, 30, 32, 33, 34
partnership with North Rhine-Westphalia 29
selection and supervision of school personnel 67–8
teachers' political role 110
Brown, A. and Gray, J. 8
Bündnis 90 28

Carnoy, M. and Levin, H. 4, 59
chemistry 32
child-centered learning 12, 16, 18, 19, 31
churches 10, 27, 33, 106
classless society 12, 13
classroom management 47 (*see also* discipline)
collectivism 12, 13
collegiality 46
competition 17, 71, 73
comprehensive school *see Gesamtschule*
conservative policies 10, 89
Cuban, L. 4, 22, 59
curriculum 12, 15
  astronomy 34
  democratization 44–7, 56
  higher education 92, 95, 98–9
  reform in Brandenburg 22–4
  assimilation versus differentiation 35–7
  chemistry 32
  departure from GDR traditions 24–5
  foreign language teaching 26, 27–8
  Gesellschaftskunde (societal education) 25–6
  Lebenskunde-Ethik-Religion (LER) 32, 33, 106
  Leistungsklassen (achievement classes) 26
  new subjects 32
  philosophy 32–3
  public consultation 27–8

129

Index

religious instruction 28
school week 26, 27
subject matter frameworks 30–31, 34
teacher training 34–5
traditional subjects 31–2
three-tier secondary school structure 63
vocational education 34

Dalton, R. 3
democratization 2
  abuse of freedom 41, 44
  civic culture 4, 37
  classroom management 47 (see also discipline)
  curriculum 44–7, 56
  disillusionment 52–3, 55
  meritocracy 9, 43, 72, 78, 80, 89
  new laws and directives 47–8, 56
  parents' rights 41, 56
  school reform acts 39
  shared authority 37, 56
  teachers 37–9
    political role 50–55, 110
discipline 40, 41, 43, 47, 49, 75–6, 84, 87
disillusionment 52–3, 55

Eastern Germany
  Brandenburg see Brandenburg
  Bündnis 90 28
  classless society 12, 13
  democratization see democratization
  economic transformation 108
  educational reform 4–5
    assimilation versus differentiation 104–5
    excellence versus equity 106
    ideas shared with the West 34
    lack of coherence 106
    schools as symbols of continuity 109
    teachers' reactions 107–8
  educational system
    adoption of three-tier secondary schools 19, 20–21, 30, 58 (see also Brandenburg; Thüringen)
    anti-fascism 12–13
    collectivism 12, 13
    comparison with the West 8–9, 49
    competition 17
    curriculum see curriculum
    Erweiterte Oberschule (extended secondary school) 13–14, 58, 76, 78–9
    higher education see higher education
    ideological conflict 16–17
    militarization 15
    policy-making 14–15
    Polytechnische Oberschule (unitary polytechnical school) 13–14, 42, 58
    social levelling 71–2, 74
    retention of teaching staff 2, 3, 109
    student failure 72, 78–9, 84
    teachers' authority 40
    teachers' autonomy 15–16
    Thüringen see Thüringen
    unification with the West 17–21, 104
    university entrance 14, 92
  federalism 4
  fertility rates 2, 79
  first state elections 28
  Round Tables 18, 27
  Socialist Unitary Party (SED) 14, 25, 26, 28
  unemployment 2, 108
  unification 2–3
educational reform 4–5
  assimilation versus differentiation 104–5
  curriculum see curriculum
  democratization see democratization
  excellence versus equity 106
  lack of coherence 106
  schools as symbols of continuity 109
  teachers' reactions 107–8, 111–12
educational standards 76–9, 86–7
elections 28
elitism 10–11
Elmore, R. and Sykes, G. 5, 59
employment prospects 2, 73–4
engineering 92, 98, 99
EOS see Erweiterte Oberschule
equity 106
Erweiterete Oberschule (extended secondary school) 13–14, 58, 76, 78–9
ethical education 32, 33, 106
excellence 106

failure rates 72, 78–9, 84
Fachhochschulen 92, 95, 98
federalism 4, 11, 96, 100
  levels of government 60–62
Fend, H. 5
fertility rates 2, 79
Finley, M. 59
Fischer, A. 13, 14, 15
Fishman, S. and Martin, L. 8, 10
foreign language teaching 26, 27–8, 82
freedom of speech 9, 39
Friedeburg, L.V. 10, 12
Frühwald, W. et al. 98
Fullan, M. 5, 38

Index

GDR (German Democratic Republic) *see* Eastern Germany
Geißler, R. 14
German Democratic Republic (GDR) *see* Eastern Germany
Germany
  East *see* Eastern Germany
  West *see* Western Germany
Gesamtschule (comprehensive school) 10, 30
  Brandenburg 64–6, 69, 70, 82–4, 85–6, 88
Gesellschaftskunde (societal education) 25–6
Giesen, B. and Leggewie, K. 3
government agencies 60–62, 66–7, 71
Green Party (*Die Grünen*) 62
Grüner, P. 18, 25
Guttmann, A. 37, 56
Gymnasium 10–11, 30
  Brandenburg 64–5, 69, 70, 74–81
  gauging standards 76
  status of teachers 79–80
  student body composition 74–6
  Thüringen 62, 63, 64, 69–70, 74–81
  upholding standards 77–9

Habel, W., Hansen, R., Krampe, C., Portz, S. and Spies, W. 59
Hauptschule 10, 11
  proposed in Brandenburg 85
  Thüringen 62, 63, 64, 84
Hearnden, A. 8, 14, 15
Heinrich, H. 19
Hemmings, A. and Metz, M. 59
higher education (*see also* university entrance)
  GDR system 91–2
  reconstruction 90–91
  curricula and examination requirements 95, 98–9
  legal framework 96
  new *Fachhochschulen* 92, 95, 98
  new universities 97
  number of institutions 95
  role of the *Strukturkommissionen* (planning commissions) 93, 94
  role of the *Wissenschaftsrat* (scientific council) 93, 96–8
  staff recruitment 99–100
  standardization of East and West 95–6, 100–101
  research 91, 94
Honecker, Margot 25, 27
Huberman, M. and Miles, M. 5
humanities 92, 98, 99

individualism 9

Kaack, H. 19
Keddie, N. 59
Kiefer, P. 16
Kienitz, V. 19
Klemm, K., Böttcher, W. and Weegen, M. 79
Klier, F. 14, 16, 18
König, H.J. 18
language teaching 26, 27–8, 82
Lebenskunde-Ethik-Religion (LER) 32, 33
Leistungsklassen (achievement classes) 26
Lemke, C. 14, 17, 89
Lepenies, W. 13
literature 49, 52
Little, J. 59
Little, J. and McLaughlin, M. 38
local government 60–62, 66–7, 71
Lortie, D. 88

Marsh, D. and Odden, A. 5
Marxism-Leninism 15, 25, 92
McLaughlin, M. 5
meritocracy 9, 43, 72, 78, 80, 89
Metz, M. 59
Meumann, E. 20
Meyer, H.J. 19
Meyer, J. 59
Meyer, J. and Rowan, B. 5
military instruction 15, 92
Mintrop, H. and Weiler, H. 59
Mitter, Wolfgang 8, 20
moral education 32, 33, 106
Mostyn, B. 39
Müller, B. 19

numerus clausus 92

Oakes, J. 59
Oakes, J., Gamoran, A. and Page, R. 59
O'Donnell, G. and Schmitter, P. 2, 20, 37
Offe, C. 3
Okun, B. 18
Oswald, H., Baker, D. and Stevenson, D. 59

Pädagogisches Landesinstitut Brandenburg (PLIB) 29, 30, 32, 33, 34
Page, R. and Valli, L. 59
parents 11, 12, 16, 18, 40, 110
  choice of secondary school
    Brandenburg 64, 65, 69, 70, 75
    Thüringen 62, 63, 69, 75

131

Index

increased rights 41, 56
relationship with teachers 41–2
paternalism 42, 55–6
Philipp, E. and Witjes, W. 10, 59
philosophy 32–3
pluralism 9, 39
Pollack, D. 3
Polytechnische Oberschule (unitary polytechnical school) 13–14, 42, 58
POS *see Polytechnische Oberschule*
principals 54–5
  selection and supervision 68
progressive policies 9–10, 29, 31, 34

Realschule 10, 11, 30
  Brandenburg 64, 65, 69, 70, 83
  Thüringen 62, 63, 64, 84
reform *see* educational reform
Regelschule 62–4, 69–70, 81–2, 84–5, 88
religious discrimination 40, 52
religious instruction 28, 33
research 91, 94
Rist, R. 59
Round Tables 18, 27
Rudolf, R. 16
Russian language 26

Sarason, S.B. 5, 59
Schmidt, G. 18
Schmidt, W. 2, 18
school administration 60–62, 66–7, 71
school principals 54–5
  selection and supervision 68
school week 26, 27
schools
  democratization *see* democratization
  secondary *see* secondary schools
  symbols of continuity 109
Schreiner, M. 18
Schwerin, E. 28
Schwille, J. *et al.* 5, 59
science education 26, 31, 48–9
  chemistry 32
  engineering 92, 98, 99
secondary schools
  Erweiterte Oberschule (extended secondary school) 13–14, 58, 76, 78–9
  Gesamtschule (comprehensive school) 10, 30
    Brandenburg 64–6, 69, 70, 82–4, 85–6, 88
  Gymnasium 10–11, 30
    Brandenburg 64–5, 69, 70, 74–81
    gauging standards 76

status of teachers 79–80
student body composition 74–6
Thüringen 62, 63, 64, 69–70, 74–81
upholding standards 77–9
Hauptschule 10, 11
  proposed in Brandenburg 85
  Thüringen 62, 63, 64, 84
Polytechnische Oberschule (unitary polytechnical school) 13–14, 42, 58
Realschule 10, 11, 30
  Brandenburg 64, 65, 69, 70, 83
  Thüringen 62, 63, 64, 84
Regelschule 62–4, 69–70, 81–2, 84–5, 88
selective education 10
social levelling 71–2, 74
Socialist Unity Party (SED) 14, 25, 26, 28
Sorensen, A. 59
standards 76–9, 96–7
Steffens, U. and Bargel, T. 5
Strukturkommissionen (planning commissions) 93, 94
student-centered learning 12, 16, 18, 19, 31
student failure 72, 78–9 84

Talbert, J. 59
teacher training 34–5
teachers
  authority 40, 56
  autonomy 12, 15–16
  collegiality 46
  competence
    discipline 40, 41, 43, 47, 49, 75–6, 84, 87
    East-West comparisons 49, 56
    new laws and directives 47–8, 56
    new subject matter 44–7, 56
    staff development 49–50
    subject knowledge 48–50, 56
  democratization *see* democratization
  disillusionment 52–3, 55
  insecurity 53, 56–7
  job security 109–10
  paternalism 42, 55–6
  political role 16, 50–55, 110
  reactions to educational changes 107–8, 111–12
  relationship with parents 41–2
  relationship with students 42–3, 112
  retention 2, 3, 109
  selection and supervision 67–8
  status in the *Gymnasium* 79–80
  submissiveness 53–4, 55

132

Index

Thüringen
　adoption of three-tier secondary schools 58–60, 66
　acceptance of tracking 71–4
　creation of the *Regelschule* 62–4, 69–70, 81–2, 84–5, 88
　government agencies 60–62, 66–7, 71
　lower track schools 84–8
　status of the *Gymnasium* 74–81
　proposed European University in Erfurt 97
　selection and supervision of school personnel 67–8
　teachers' political role 110
Tiefensee, E. 28

Uhlig, G. 15
unemployment 2, 108
unification 2–3, 17–21
university entrance 9, 10, 11, 14, 63
　(*see also* higher education)

vocational education 9, 10, 34
Von Beyme, K. 3

Weiler, H. 10, 22, 55, 59
Weick, K. 59
Western Germany
　educational system
　　comparison with the East 8–9, 49
　　conservative policies 10
　　curriculum 12
　　federalism 11, 96, 100
　　ideas shared with the East 34
　　individualism 9
　　meritocracy 9
　　pluralism 9
　　progressive policies 9–10
　　social reconstruction 9
　　state control 11–12
　　student-centered learning 12
　　teachers' autonomy 12
　　three-tier structure 10, 19
　　university entrance 9, 10, 11
Wirt, F. and Kirst, M. 59
Wissenschaftsrat (scientific council) 93, 96–8
Wolf, Christa 18

Zapf, W. 2, 55

133

For Product Safety Concerns and Information please contact our EU
representative GPSR@taylorandfrancis.com
Taylor & Francis Verlag GmbH, Kaufingerstraße 24, 80331 München, Germany

www.ingramcontent.com/pod-product-compliance
Lightning Source LLC
Chambersburg PA
CBHW050556300426
44112CB00013B/1942